THE SHIFTING PARADYM OF OUR FRACTURED COUNTRY

(MANKIND'S NEXT

GREAT ADVANCE)

DOUGLAS F. SCHROEDER

ISBN: 13 978-1717352729

10-1717352723

LIBRARY OF CONGRESS NUMBER

Published by: Amazon Books

First printing of this book – 2018

Order additional copies of this book from:

Amazonbooks.com or createspace.com

The cover picture depicts the sunrise over a serene lake

indicating the dawning of a kinder and more gentle world.

ACKNOWLEDGMENTS

First and primarily I would like to thank my wife, Loretta, for the many hours she spent proofreading and reviewing my work. She provided me with many suggestions and grammar corrections which definitely made this a much better book. Thank you, Loretta.

TABLE OF CONTENTS

SECTION I THE MENTAL COMPONENT

Mankind's Mental and Personal Relations

SECTION II THE PHYSICAL COMPONENT

The Physical Universe

SECTION III THE SPIRIT COMPONENT

The Spirit Universe

INTRODUCTION

Our country seems riddled with problems, which seem to be tearing us apart and making life difficult. A major issue we have in resolving many of these problems is our inability to determine exactly what the problem really is and trying to phrase it in such a way so that everyone interprets it in the same way. Vaguely stated problems are difficult, if not impossible, to resolve. Unless we can resolve these problems or at least change how we address them, our future is in jeopardy. Also, in the future, additional problems will be added to the list of current problems, including items such as global warming, sea level rise, severe weather, water and food shortages in various parts of the world, mass migration of people, and many other problems requiring not only national unity but international cooperation. The world will be looking to the United States for leadership, whether we want to lead or not. Thus it is imperative that we first get our own house in order. I am concentrating on a few problems of my country, the USA, mainly because I am certainly more familiar with my own country. Thus, I'm staying away from directly including all people in this analysis. However, as the saying goes, "If the shoe fits, wear it!"

The problems which I discuss are not necessarily the primary problems we face, merely problems which I felt needed to be considered and discussed. Also they are not listed in order of importance or any order in particular. In many cases I have restated the problem to make it more amenable to resolution. I do not even attempt to discuss all of our problems, but I believe that I do discuss enough of them to indicate at least a partial resolution.

This book is divided into three parts:

Section I - The Mental Component as I call it, which is the power of our mind and our relationships.

Section II - The Physical Component, which is the environment in which we live.

Section III –The Spirit Component, which we will inhabit once we leave the physical world.

In my discussions of religion oriented problems, I must of necessity rely on my knowledge of the Christian religion. It is my religion and is considered the primary religion of our nation. It is the one with which I am most familiar. While I am not well versed on the other religions of the world, I suspect that their basic tenets are probably not much different from each other or from Christianity so as to invalidate what I have to say.

I did not do any special research for this book. I think the facts are generally current, but I certainly do not guarantee them, nor will I defend them as factual items, since facts can be and are determined in different ways by different people; therefore, it would be useless to debate them. For those of you who want facts, you can do your own research.. Thus, in general, I have stated my knowledge and beliefs rather than published facts.

I not only itemize some details about these problems, but I may also restate the problem and usually also propose a possible solution. This does not indicate that I believe that this is the only solution, but should be taken as a discussion point which should lead to a solution. Many of my conclusions and proposed solutions will seem far out and strange. However, if we look at our country, we will quickly note that we cannot continue on the path we are following and that it will require some far reaching and new ways to resolve these problems. Since I did not do a lot of research before embarking on this project, it is primarily a compilation of my own experiences and knowledge which I have amassed during my lifetime, and of course my personal ideas of what should be done. In some cases I also try to define why we have such divergent opinions on what should be done. I encourage you to read it with an open mind and defer judgement until you have finished the book.

Some people think that all of our troubles signify the downfall of our country, just as with The Roman Empire, which some say was destroyed by internal troubles. I do not agree with this analysis; actually I think these troubles are the precursor to another major change in human nature. To accomplish this change in human behavior, we must overcome these problems. As I see it, this change in human nature will result in a "kinder, gentler humanity." See Section II for more information on major shifts in human nature.

OUR USE OF MIND-ALTERING DRUGS

This is a very complicated area in which to get involved. We could include alcoholic beverages with this category, but that in itself is such a large area I shall treat it separately, later in this chapter. However, we shall include everything from marijuana to the standard drugs such as heroin, synthetic drugs, prescription drugs and anything that now or in the future fits the definition of mind-altering and is being used for recreational purposes.

This has always been a problem in our society, in fact probably in all or most societies. The real problem is that it seems to have become much more serious. One reason is the easy availability and the reduced cost for obtaining drugs. They are shipped worldwide to anyplace where they can be sold. Let's face it: we have the money, and we purchase them. We are a very profitable market for the makers and sellers of these mind-altering drugs. We spend untold amounts of money, effort, and time trying to stop the flow of these items. Since it is such a lucrative business, we cannot stop the flow of them. It will only stop when we stop purchasing them. Thus, our efforts must be concentrated in stopping the use of them. Only then will the flow of these items stop.

So, why do we use mind-altering drugs for recreational purposes? This is not a new behavior but has been a problem for mankind for most of our history. However, it seems to be at epidemic levels, and we are increasingly trying to make the use of some substances legal for recreational purposes. Thus we need to determine the reasons for drug usage for recreational uses. Of course, when people are beset with problems and are unable to solve them or live with them, they often turn to drugs for relief. However, this does not solve their problem, but just exchanges one problem for another; it merely exasperates the problem. Today many think that we should not have to suffer, life should be all fun. Of course that is impossible, so we often turn to drugs to alter our minds in such a way so as to make it seem possible. Other people get hooked on drugs while using them for medical reasons or are talked into trying them by peer pressure. Once a person is addicted, many will do most anything to get that next fix.

This drug addiction is not only a problem for young people, but affects people of all ages, the rich and the poor, educated and uneducated, and people in most all occupations. Thus, it is a national problem and has national consequences. It has the potential of bringing a nation to its knees. Large sums of money are spent not only in trying to control the drug problem, but also in trying to cure the addicted, paying for illnesses they contact because of the drug usage, for taking care of them when they are no longer able to take care of themselves, and paying for the damage and crimes they commit while under the influence of drugs. This includes many deaths caused by them under the influence, such as car accidents and crimes committed to obtain money to feed their habit. Many other direct and indirect costs are associated with the influence of drugs.

So what can or should we do about this problem? Up until now we have mostly tried punishment, spent exorbitant amounts of money on trying to stop the flow of the drugs, and tried mainly voluntary education. We seem to have achieved no or only minimal success with these methods. So what else can we do? First of all, we must look at the reasons why people turn to drugs. It seems to be primarily to change our outlook of the world and/or of ourselves. We are just not satisfied with the situation, in which we find ourselves, with ourselves or how we are living our lives. We grow up thinking and believing that we should be able to control the world around us and make it an ever joyous environment. When we find out that this is not possible, we try to find ways to make it fit our expectations. Often this involves altering our mind with drugs. Basically it means changing our outlook on life itself; however, it is we the people who must change. See the chapter on "Raising Children" for further information.

Instead of reducing our use of drugs, we are actually trying to make the recreational use of drugs legal and easier to obtain. Some states already have shops which can sell marijuana for recreational purposes and are probably good money makers. I suspect that this is just the opening salvo to make drugs universally legally available for recreational use. Where is this leading us? I fear the long term results of this. Drug use has become a major killer in our society. How many of our fellow human beings must be killed before we take action? Somehow we must solve this problem before it overtakes us.

What we must do is take away a person's most prized possessions and then retrain that person. Under no circumstances can we allow drug dealers, transporters and manufacturers to make a profit or retain assets from their illegal dealing in drugs. What we must do is immediately take away a person's most prized possessions, money, and power, and then retrain that person as soon as we arrest someone making, transporting, or selling drugs. We must confiscate all of their assets and take away their family. I don't think anyone can make a case that people are good for their families while involved with the trafficking of drugs. They will then need to be retrained in working for a living without dealing in drugs. Drug users will go through mandatory detox and education training until they are cured. All users, dealers, and manufacturers must be certified as cured before they can return to society. See the chapter on "Our Justice System" for more information.

Now let us turn our attention to the alcohol problem we face. This is not much different from the drug problem discussed above. It is more prevalent and is engraved in all aspects and people in our society. It has most of the same causes discussed above for the drug problem but is much more sensitive to peer pressure. It is not considered by our society as being as bad as drug use; in fact, it is considered as being just part of our lives. Drinking, even by minors, which is illegal, seems to be overlooked by the police unless it causes other laws to be broken. So with all of us looking the other way and ignoring it, it continues, or even gets to be a more serious. So what are some of the causes of this dilemma?

We are bombarded by all of our communications media about alcohol. Not only are products very highly advertised, but their use is displayed, especially in our entertainment media. Many of our celebrities and/or famous personalities are shown using it and even promoting it. Many business people, politicians, government workers, and entertainment people admit to using drugs and/or alcohol in excess. Thus it covers the spectrum of our society. I remember one famous person, when asked why he always seemed to be drinking on the show, stated that it was just social drinking. Of course, social drinking has about as many definitions as there are drinkers. Some people do their social drinking while staggering about at 1:00 AM. The other problem with calling it social drinking, is that it allows people to drink at any time: while on the air or television, while interacting with friends or business associates, or merely relaxing at home with family members. While social drinking is thus just a term to make drinking acceptable, actually I think it promotes drinking. Admittedly, all kinds of alcoholic beverages are advertised by all available media and are readily available. Of course they have disclaimers to cover themselves, but those are probably not read by anyone except the lawyers. They are not reaching and affecting minors, addicts, and almost everybody else with their message. It is probably impossible to not be influenced by these ads. But, we can't seem to be able to interfere with businesses' rights to make money in any way they desire or can; we can only be quiet and pay for the damage drinking does. We also seem inclined to punish the alcohol pushers and dealers with a slap on the wrist, while we often send the end users to jail. That, for the most part, has proven ineffective. Of course children take their behavior cues from their parents, and I would estimate that most of us parents are "social" drinkers or even heavy drinkers especially on weekends. So what will the kids be when they grow up? Again, the causes for alcohol usage and addiction are probably the same as drug usage discussed above. It seems that it is easier to ignore alcohol abuse since it is not considered as bad as drug usage, and is also considered more acceptable to society. We feel that alcohol enhances our ability to have and enjoy pleasure. Thus it is widely used. We are tempted with alcohol from a very early age. Our parents use it and enjoy it, friends and neighbors use it and always seem to enjoy it. Then comes peer pressure which promotes the attitude that we are not part of the group or participating in the party or group activity if we don't drink. Pretty soon we are drinking, too!

So what makes drinking different today? For one thing, we seem to need or want to drink as much as possible as quickly as possible. We chug-a-lug our drinks, pour them directly down our throats, go from bar to bar drinking at each one, and keep ordering stronger and stronger drinks as the evening progresses. We go out drinking with the plan to pass out drunk before the evening is over. Even more alarming is the fact that girls are now often doing the same thing. They used to act as the brakes to male drinking, not that this was their responsibility, but now they are joining the men in this outrageous drinking, often with dire consequences. The consequences of alcohol use are much the same as the consequences of using drugs. The primary consequences we see with alcohol usage seem to be in the problems it causes with driving, in our sexual drive, and in our relationships with other people.

So what can we do with the habitual offenders of alcoholic beverages and drugs? First of all, we must institute a mandatory detox and a training session for these people requiring that they could only be released when certified cured. For additional infractions, tougher measures must be taken. When we must not allow these offenders to drive a vehicle when they are in treatment. Once they are deemed cured, they could be allowed to drive again. We cannot afford to allow these habitual drunks with multiple DUIs to continue to endanger themselves and other drivers on the road. For those offenders with inappropriate behavior, we must institute new training procedures and detention methods. See the chapters on "Education" and "Our Justice System" for more information. Of course we tried outlawing alcohol, and it naturally failed miserably. Again, drugs and alcohol are primarily a moral problem, not only a legal problem.

Finally, I turn attention to the tobacco problem. It may not exactly fit in this chapter, but it is closely related, so I will include it. This category includes smoking and chewing tobacco as well as the new nicotine smoking devices which are gaining popularity.

Smoking can be highly addictive; in fact, some scientists deem it more addictive than drugs or alcohol. It is very difficult to make it illegal or tax it enough to force people to quit. These measures can, of course, have their own side effects causing other problems. It is a very difficult problem, as are most behavioral problems, and thus must in the final analysis be overcome by each individual. The effects of nicotine are probably more medical related rather than psychological. However, we must keep in mind that we are all individuals and vary a lot in our personal addiction. It is a very difficult problem, as are most behavioral problems, and thus must in the final analysis be overcome by each individual. The desire to smoke/chew tobacco and how prone we are to becoming addicted to nicotine is different for each individual. Thus, a single cure for nicotine usage will only work for a subset of users.

So what can we, as concerned individuals, do to stem this trend? First of all, we must set the example for others and discourage these actions rather than encourage them. Also, we must stop patronizing people who foster and encourage these actions by not supporting their businesses. Cutting off their profits can go a long way to discourage these businesses. Moderation is the key to alcohol use and for most, if not all, recreational drugs I suspect that complete abstinence is the only answer for drug addicts. . Violators must be retrained and given a new lifestyle, and they must be made to understand that second chances are probably not available.

So what are our options for resolving this manifold problem? We could ignore it and continue to let it haunt us.

or

 We could ban all of these products, but it would most likely fail just like prohibition failed the last time we tried it.

or

We could try to severely limit the use of the liquors with a high alcohol content. It is probably the consumption of this liquor that causes most of our liquor problems; thus, we must learn how to control the usage of it. Also, it is this liquor that is often consumed with the objective of becoming drunk. We probably can't outlaw it, so it must be controlled by education and technology, which will also help control other alcoholic beverages. We must increase our control of all drugs so we would not be able to use them for recreational purposes. Along with that, we should use the latest and best detox methods to cure abusers of alcohol and drugs. We should start education for this in earnest in the low primary grades and continue it through all schooling and in conjunction with detox. We must monitor and control the sale of liquor and drugs. We must also limit the amount of low alcohol content liquor. While legal means can help us in controlling drug usage, liquor and tobacco usage is very difficult to control by legal means. These will have to be controlled primarily by a change in human nature, i.e. we must begin to lead more Christian lives and learn to control ourselves. We must learn that we really don't need alcohol to be happy and have fun.

This would the preferred Christian answer.

WOMEN'S LIB

This is a problem that has been brewing for a very long time. The core of the problem is the desire of women to be equal to their male counterparts: politically, socially, and economically. It also extends into the areas of education, sports, entertainment and opportunity in all aspects of life. It certainly was the correct thing to do, but it was a long time in coming, and we still aren't quite there. While we are still fighting this problem, I must say that we have made significant progress.

The first major breakthrough came when women gained the right to vote. All of a sudden they controlled about half of the vote, both nationally and on the local level. This gave them the ability to push their agenda by being able to control who our political representatives would be. Now the politicians had to listen and act or be voted out of office. After that, things started to change more rapidly, but not all at once. It still took a lot of work and demonstrations to get these changes enacted.

The middle of the last century was a time of intense activity, and a lot of the gains made were initiated during this era. There now were many more women entering politics and winning, even at the national level. The number of women in political office still is not nearly representative of their percentage of the population; however, they have certainly made gains and will continue to make gains. We have not yet elected a female president, but in 2016 there was a women running for that office as the representative of one of the major political parties and, even though she lost in the Electoral College vote, she did get more than one half of the popular vote. Women are now the CEOs of a few major corporations and continue to obtain many top positions in major corporations. So their power and influence continue to grow.

In other areas the progress is spottier. There is still a differential in wages for various reasons. Again some progress is being made, in sports for example; I believe that this past year the purses for both men's and women's top winners in tennis have been made equal. We still have a discrepancy in childcare responsibilities. Benefits for the sexes are not always the same. There still seems to be a gap in the opportunities available between the sexes. There are many more areas of inequity, but we are making progress and must continue to work for complete equality.

Unfortunately, with such gains we must also contend with the negative aspects that came with those gains. As good as those gains are, the negatives are also bad, and we must deal with them.

Some of the proponents of women's lib were not satisfied with either the goals or progress of the movement. This probably is the younger segment of the movement. They were looking for not only equality with their male counterparts, but also to be the same as they were. Perhaps, they noted that men were still having more fun and enjoyment in life and also wanted some of that for themselves. I think this reinvigorated the "girls just want to have fun" movement. While the attitude of being the same does have some merit, I surly hope this never materializes, for we really have enough problems when we are different, and being the same would just increase our problems. It would surely be a dull world if we were all the same.

Girls now party like and with the boys and follow their lead in raising hell. Some curse and use coarse language like the boys, and some are worse than the boys. Some drink like the boys; they drink a lot of liquor fast, just like the boys at a frat party. Since their tolerance for alcohol is generally less than for boys, they often get drunk before the boys which often allow the boys to have their way. We find them in groups or sitting alone in the bar to pick up boys or to be picked up by boys. Some go out to drink with the expressed purpose of getting passed out drunk which can end up with dire consequences. Many now participate in behavior they never used to.

During this time period the development of the birth control pill and the morning after pill to a large extent freed girls from the pregnancy consequences; thus, many now feel free to have sex at will. As far as having fun, they seem to be much more equal with the boys.

Another outcome of women's lib is that now everyone, especially women, is dressing more and more risqué. In fact many, especially celebrities, are now shedding all of their clothes, having pictures taken in various poses, and even in performing various sex acts and publishing them on the internet or in various magazines. Another technique often used is to not wear any underwear and then "accidently" expose their genitals for the troops of cameramen following them. This exposure is not only popular with entertainment celebrities, but with other well-known people, and the want-to-be celebrities. Perhaps they think that their bodies are so great that they have to share them with the whole world and make them available to posterity. A current incident in the Marines and the other military branches highlights this problem. Women and even men are now appearing nude or in other compromising positions on social media, and the culprits who then release these pictures to the public, probably mostly men, were blamed as they probably should be. But looking at the other side of this problem, as we should, why were those nude pictures available? Certainly they were not all stolen, and even those which were stolen, why were these pictures taken and available? They couldn't all have been taken surreptitiously. So a lot of blame must also go to those posing nude, although the primary blame must fall on those who posted them.

There seems to be a heated argument in this area. Some women are arguing that since men are allowed to go topless in public, they too should be allowed to do the same. Other women are dead set against this further exposure of their bodies. I think most women are concerned that men's first attention is on their breasts and genitals. My take on this matter is that going topless will increase men's attention on their genitals and breasts instead of on them as persons. If men going topless has the same effect on women as does women going topless has on men, then perhaps men should not go topless.

As Christians we must continue to strive for equality between the sexes and for all people and attempt to minimize the associated problems. We must work on the associated problems and minimize their influence. We must not exacerbate the problem by what we do, how we dress, and how we talk.

or

We can continue with what we are doing and continue dealing with these problems.

MEDICAL DILEMMA

What is happening to what we so fondly call the best medical system in the world? People from all over the world are coming to our medical facilities and specialists to get treatment for illnesses for which they are unable to get anywhere else in the world, although there are more places in the world who are beginning to provide the same expert medical service. However, this is just one part of the equation. The other part involves the question as to who can have access to this excellent medical expertise.

We will take a quick look at the development of our medical service. In the last 75 years our medical system has undergone some major changes. Doctors, probably most of them, were general practitioners who pretty much treated all illnesses and rarely referred patients to a specialist, if one was even available. They knew their patients very well and could quickly determine what was going on with them. Hospitals were generally local and staffed by volunteers, such as religious organizations whose sisters received little or no pay. Drugs were dispensed by local drug stores that were able to keep the cost of drugs reasonable. The pharmaceutical companies were providing a smaller number of drugs that were cheaper to manufacture. Research on new drugs was much cheaper, and not as many new drugs were being developed.

One of the biggest and most important developments was the introduction of medical insurance. It enabled people to share in the cost of medical treatment. Later, drugs were added to medical insurance. Actually, with co-payments, initial self-payments, policy maximums, sickness exclusions, pre-existing exclusions, and who knows what all, it was confusing to policyholders and hard to determine what was covered and what was not. All this required insurance companies to have huge staffs, and they developed into another large industry that had to be supported by medical costs without any direct benefit to one's health. So in total, the cost of medical care increased.

At the same time, the hospital industry was also changing. Business was recognizing that hospitals could be huge profit centers, and business started buying and building hospitals. Subsequently, hospitals were run as a business for profit; no longer were they primarily for the welfare of the sick. Cost cutting became a standard operating procedure sometimes at the cost of welfare to the patients. For better or worse, most patients now spend less time in the hospital. Fewer highly trained personnel are hired and cheaper personnel are hired. We still have a lot of highly trained personnel who love their job and deeply care for their patients. But, we also have more workers who are there just to collect their monthly paychecks.

Meanwhile, the family doctors started to organize into larger and larger clinics with multiple doctors and an increasing number of staff members for support services. Also, these clinics are staffed with an increasing number of specialists in order to provide a one-stop service for their patients. Thus, referrals to other clinics are not always necessary. However these specialists also combined to form specialty clinics. All in all, our medical services changed greatly during this time.

Meanwhile, the pharmaceutical industry was not sitting by idly. They were developing new drugs at a record pace.

Since it was so profitable, they continued to expand, producing more and more drugs.

They have always had drug reps who visited the various medical facilities and providers to convince them to use the drugs their company manufactured. Now they have expanded into advertising to convince patients to ask the doctor for their drugs; however, they call it "educating the public." They greatly expanded their research into new drugs, and with new technology, the cost of this research increased significantly.

Although with all these changes, we probably did not get the personal attention we were accustomed to, we probably got better drugs. As a result, we got increased medical costs which increased every year. In fact, the prices were going up so much that an increasing number of people could no longer afford medical care. This is when the government stepped in to assist the lower classes with their medical bills. First, Medicaid and Medicare were established. Later, drugs were added to Medicare. Finally, too many people were not able to afford medical insurance and thus Obamacare was instituted, primarily as an assist in buying medical insurance. While it certainly had some good qualities, such as getting rid of pre-existing illness clauses, eliminating maximum total payments by insurance companies, and providing allowances to insure one's children to age 26, the remainder of the bill was a series of compromises between the two political parties and thus nobody was happy with the medical coverage. Consequently, Obamacare became a monster which did little to slow the rate of medical costs for the consumers. Now the government is again looking at a new bill to hopefully correct the inadequacies of the Obama bill.

So what is the cause of the drastic increases in medical cost? Actually every sector of the medical system has to bear some responsibility for these rising costs. First of all, the medical clinics became big business with a lot of overhead and operating expenses. Today the doctors have a choice of many more procedures and tools to diagnose and treat patients and often are required to use more than they would normally use because of protocols required by the clinic administration. Often these additional tests are used to cover the doctor and clinics in case of a lawsuit. Also, many doctors, especially specialists, are paid wages much higher than we would expect. Some are so far out of line that we must wonder if they can really relate to their patients. Of course, I suspect that the clinic administrators and other high level administrators perhaps are paid even more. Really who needs these exorbitant wages and benefits to help their fellow human beings? For hospitals we could list the same problems.

Additionally, the drug industry has its own problems. It blames the high cost of drugs on the cost of research to test and bring new drugs to the market. Of course that cost must be borne by the sale of existing drugs. I have two problems with this reasoning. First of all, what all is included in these research and development costs? We, the consumers, really don't know, so we do not know if these costs are allocated fairly. Secondly should most of the cost come from the sale of existing drugs to citizens of our country, or should more of the cost be allocated to other countries that use drugs manufactured by these same companies? Also, should we be able to use drugs manufactured by other countries that make the same drugs and comply with our standards? What about the gigantic price increases in drugs that have been on the market for a long time? Are drug companies just padding their bottom line by charging a captive consumer base exorbitant prices? I think we should also ask why some of these CEOs are earning millions of dollars off the back of poorer people. Are their workers and scientists earning fair wages for the work they do to help the less fortunate? Are their advertising and sales methods really fair for the products they sell? These are valid concerns that should be addressed.

Another real problem is that we seem to be wide open to charlatans practicing unorthodox medicine promising cures to helpless people desperately looking for a cure. Also, we must revamp our legal system concerning medical lawsuits. See the chapter on "Our Legal System."

Finally, we the people must change our attitude toward medical care. We expect that there is a pill available to cure any illness we have. We think that we should be able to make it through life with no or only a minimal amount of suffering. We tell the doctor what medicine he should prescribe to cure our ailments. Take antibiotics for instance: we want an antibiotic even if it won't help us at all, even though we have been warned for years that overuse of these will make them ineffective.

For the future we must maintain our world leadership in medical care, and at the same time we must make it available and affordable for all of our citizens. Personally, I think affordable medical care is a right for all of our citizens. In order to meet these goals, we must resolve all the problems mentioned above. This will not be easy since it means resolving a lot of other problems which will be brought up later in this book.

Mental health, too, is an area that requires a lot of attention in our society. Currently mental health is often ignored or given short shrift in our society. Too often mental patients are admitted for treatment, treated for a few days, and then released back into society before they are cured. Thus they are back to fighting the same problems they had, putting not only themselves in danger, but also society at large. We must change our attitude about mental health and realize that by investing money in curing mental illness, we could save a lot of collateral expenses, personal tragedy, threats to society, and improving the quality of the sufferers. We cannot ignore it, hoping that it will go away. Somehow we must find a way of providing medical care to all of our people rather than sliding into the abyss of providing excellent medical care to those who have the money while providing only minimal care for the remainder of the population. Most of our medical system will have to recognize that their primary concern must be assisting their fellow human beings, instead of believing that their patients' main business is to make them millionaires and billionaires. Unfortunately, I believe medical care has become a political football where politics is more important than helping people with their medical problems. Until the politicians can agree that only if they put the patients first and their political responsibilities a distant second, can we expect any improvement of our medical care!

Our lawmakers have established their own medical insurance plan which is probably the best anywhere, at least in the United States. To be fair, they should come under the same insurance plan they provide for their constituents. Law makers are currently trying to establish a new health insurance system for their constituents. It sounds like the current pending bill they are formulating would leave millions of people uninsured and increase insurance rates. It sounds like it will leave many more people with high insurance rates which too many could not afford. Of course they would retain their very generous health insurance because they wouldn't want any part of the insurance they would provide for their constituents. There is definitely something wrong with this scenario!. As Christians, we must insist that all the people get adequate health care. We must always take care of our sick and unfortunate brethren.

So what are we going to do?

Will we continue to debate health care for who knows how long and continue to let the price of medical care continue to rise above the ability of many people to get medical care? At the same time will we continue allowing some of the rich and super rich to get even richer?

or

Can we take a more Christian approach and make sure that our sick brethren are taken care of one way or other? Decent health care must be available to all our citizens either by the generosity of all of us or through the government. I find it very difficult to watch certain people get very rich off the backs of sick people.

ABORTION CONTROVERSY

There she was, a young teen, alone, sitting on the lower step softly sobbing. She had just found out that she was pregnant. Her parents were not sympathetic at all; in fact, they berated her for her stupidity for becoming pregnant. Her boyfriend had left her all alone and didn't offer any condolence or help. She not only felt alone in this world, she indeed was all alone. She was not ready to be a mother, especially a single mother; she felt that she was still a child herself; in fact, she was still a half grown child.

Yes, she realized that she had made a mistake when she allowed her boyfriend to have intercourse with her. But don't we all make mistakes; isn't that part of being a human being? Didn't her boyfriend make exactly the same mistake? How many of us have made exactly the same mistake? However, we didn't get caught and were lucky to not end up the same way. Even if we were able to avoid the same mistake, how strong was our temptation compared to her temptation? How can we judge her when we cannot measure the strength of her temptation; are we actually playing God if we do judge her? Why do we only judge her; we know it takes two to make a baby. We tend to give the guy a bye and wish him better luck next time. Thus it often becomes the girl's problem and the boy often goes on with his normal life. I remember when I was young, the guy often joined the army after getting a girl pregnant; there nobody could or would come after him. This scenario must change. For more information, see the chapters on "Raising a Family" and "Education of our Children."

So this young girl is pondering her future, and indications are that she will be alone, a single mom, most likely very poor, and trying to raise a child she is not prepared to raise. What should she do? She has basically three choices: have the child and try to raise it herself, have the child and put it up for adoption, or have an abortion. None of the choices are very appealing to her. However, she must make a decision. Since this is a chapter on abortion, let's say she chose abortion.

Let me state that I am not in favor of the abortion option. I find the procedure crude, and it usually has unwanted consequences associated with it; thus it normally is not the best option. There are many couples who want to adopt a baby which seems to be a better option. She could also choose to raise the baby herself. However, the final decision must rest with the mother. If the father agrees to shoulder the responsibility of raising the child, both emotionally and financially, then he, too, should have a voice in the decision. Otherwise it must rest with the mother.

Abortion is a hot topic in our country, both from the political side and the religious standpoint. Much of the controversy seems to stem from the question of when the fertilized egg, or the zygote, or the fetus, becomes a human being. Once it becomes a human being, abortion can be viewed as murder. Before it becomes a human being, it can be viewed as the removal of something from the mother. So when does the fetus become a human being? Although this has developed into a political issue, it in reality is a religious issue. Actually neither the religious sector nor the scientific world have been able to determine when the fertilized egg becomes a human being. This really is the key to resolving the abortion controversy.

I did not find anything in the Bible that directly mentions abortion. There are several passages that some people interpret as addressing the abortion problem, but all of them seem to require someone to interpret what it says; however, they all seem to be interpreted as the reader wants them to be interpreted. This of course leads to more questions than answers. Thus we have many arguments and disagreements concerning abortion.

Abortion was practiced before the birth of Jesus; thus, I wonder, if it was that important, why Jesus didn't address it directly?

First of all, I believe that a human being is made up of two components, the physical component and the spirit component, or as some prefer to call it, the soul. I will refer to it as the spirit component, which is the more general term. In coming up with the following conclusions concerning abortion, I kept going back and depended on my firm belief that God is not only a very reasonable being, but also a very logical being. See more about God being a very logical being in sections II and III of this book.

This brought me to the conclusion that a fetus does not become a human being until it is joined by the spirit component, which I believe happens at the time of birth. It is when the child takes its first breath that it becomes capable of interacting with the spirit component. Therefore I believe that the spirit enters the physical being when it takes its first breath and thus becomes a human being at that time. That is a logical conclusion for a couple of reasons. First of all, if it happened before birth, it would mean that the mother would be carrying two spirit beings within her. I'm not sure that that would work since she would be interacting with two spirit beings, and it is not logical that she could do this. Which one would she influence, and which spirit would influence her? Somehow I cannot follow the logic of this situation. I know many people will say that anything is possible with God, but neither the Bible nor His life indicate this kind of lack of logic.

If we look at the Bible version of the creation of Adam, it reads
Genesis 2:7 | View whole chapter | See verse in context
"And the LORD God formed man of the dust of the ground, and breathed into his nostrils, the breath of life; and man became a living soul."

Note that it says that when He breathed into his nostrils, the man became a <u>living</u> soul. It does not say he became a living man or being, but that he became a living soul. I take this to indicate that at this time the physical man and the spirit portions of the man became merged and he became a human being as we know him and as we are.

If we can agree that abortion is primarily a personal and religious matter, we can remove it from the political arena. We know that we cannot legislate morality; thus, all politicalizing does is divide us and give the politicians an excuse for not tackling other important issues. We must address this problem from the standpoint of changing the hearts and minds of people and educating them as to the consequences of the choices they may make. I think if we decide to follow this reasoning, it will be much easier to end abortion than if we try to ban it legally and call it murder.

Actually, it doesn't matter when we believe a fertilized egg becomes a human being. In any case we cannot take over God's role as the judge and condemn the girl. We can certainly judge the act of creating the child, and/or the act of abortion, but we cannot judge the girl. Also, we cannot only blame just the girl, but we must also then blame the man, who also was involved in conceiving the baby and should be equal and caretaker and have a say in the abortion question. Finally, we cannot under any circumstance punish the innocent baby by not assisting in providing for its upbringing so that the baby doesn't becomes one of our poor and/or neglected children. So what would the Christian do in this situation?

Continue to judge her, persecute her, and make sure she and her baby live in poverty forever, as we often do?

or

 Not judge her or him; leave that to God, who knows what is in their hearts and how severe the temptation was. Assist her and her baby for as long as needed? Why do we need to punish a baby who had nothing to do with it? Also, we must treat the father who sired the baby the same as we treat the mother. It will be easier to stop abortion if we do not call it murder. Also, I think we can decrease or even virtually stop abortion if we assist the girl or parents in raising this child and making sure that the child does not fall through the cracks and grow up as a poor, second-rate, uneducated person. Actually, I think most of the churches treat a convicted murderer better than they treat a girl who aborted her baby and/or the baby a single mother is trying to raise. Clergy visit murderers in prison to assist them; how many do this for girls who aborted their baby? We must learn to be Christians. See the chapter on "Raising children" for more information on this subject.

SEXUAL ORIENTATION

This is another issue that has become a major disputed point in our country. The homosexual issue has been with us for a long time and is becoming more of a problem. Now we are also dealing with the transgender, bisexual, and other sexual dilemmas. These have generally been considered personal choice items, but there has been gradual change in our understanding of these problems.

While in some cases there probably could be a personal choice, I suspect that for most people, it certainly would not be an easy choice for people falling in these categories. Previously, society was quick to condemn them, making it very difficult for them to admit these lifestyles. We must also look at reasons for people to accept these lifestyles.

First of all, there are numerous possibilities for something to go awry while the fetus is developing. There are many instances of something being out of the norm with babies before they are born. We accept these developmental problems without question. When it comes to something going wrong with the development of the sexual orientation of a fetus, we don't accept it. Also, there can be problems in the development of the chemical and hormonal balances while the baby is developing, affecting the sexuality of the person. We seem to accept these problems in most or all areas except in the area of sexuality. I don't know how we can dismiss the possibility of this. Furthermore, as a child or even a grown person, we come in contact with a lot of chemicals in our process of living. Again, they can also affect the sexual orientation of people. Also, sexual orientation could indicate a brain/neural irregularity.

I think it is time we stopped blaming the individuals with sexual orientation problems as something over which they have complete control. They probably have no more control over this than people who have other so-called defects. We must accept the fact that they know best what their sexual orientation is and we must accept them like we accept everybody else. I do not believe that we can force them to change; we have been trying this for a long time without much success. Also, we do not have to accept how they demonstrate their sexuality, but we cannot judge them because of it; only God can do this.

Most people cite the Bible as the source of their beliefs. The Bible seems to give mixed messages which are open to interpretation.   Yes, the Old Testament did condemn homosexuals. However, Christ came with a message of mercy. I think His message was basically to not accept the practice but at the same time to not judge and condemn the person. In other words, homosexual acts may be a sin, just like the sins all of us commit at any given time. Furthermore, many heterosexual couples engage in these same acts, but we do not crucify them. Why? It is not for us to determine the severity of a person's sins, but to allow them to find ways to overcome their sins. We cannot force them to overcome these sins; they must do that themselves. We can help them if they accept our help, just like we can accept or reject others' help overcoming our own sins. As Christians, I believe we must accept the New Testament teaching. We cannot judge the person, only the act. Even if we just condemn their acts, aren't all their acts which we condemn also committed by ourselves, heterosexual "normal" people who occasionally go astray and commit these acts ourselves? Is it any different if these acts are committed by people of different sexual orientation or by heterosexual humans? I think not; if it is a sin for some then, I would suspect it is a sin for all.

What would the Christian response be?

Judge the person and condemn the person to suffering here on earth.

or

Condemn acts with which we don't agree but respect the person and help that person in any way she/he desires. However, we cannot judge the person; that is reserved for God. We must accept him/her as a child of God, just as we are, who may have strayed from what we consider right, either because of illness or by choice. We have all strayed from righteousness, so how can we consider or treat them differently? We must remember that we are all children of God.

MARRIAGE AND DIVORCE

Marriage has been a hallmark of mankind for a very long time. Actually it has probably been with us, in one form or another, since men and women decided to mate for life; marriage was probably the formalization of this decision. It is also an important item in the Bible and was probably put there to make sure that the species be propagated. God would not let his most important creation die out and disappear. Although mankind could continue to propagate without marriage, I think the main concern was the wellbeing of the children. He had to make sure that the children were taken care of and properly raised and educated. What better way to assure this than to make their creators, men and women, responsible for their children through their being married? However, this would mean that the marriage would last a very long time, perhaps even forever.

Does this have any bearing on the definition of marriage and who can be married? I think it does. If marriage is primarily for the propagation of the species and the welfare of the children, then that would mean that only a man and a women could be married. What about the other portion of our population? How about the male/male, the female/female and the other possible combinations we can have? Although for the most part they probably cannot create children, some of them are, however, raising adopted children, and some of them seem to be doing a good job of it. However, the long term results still need to be demonstrated. In my mind, I think children raised by a team composed of a male and female is still the best.

However, these other groups are still seeking equality with their heterosexual counterparts. They think that by allowing their union to be called a marriage, that will provide them with this equality. The word marriage has developed a specific meaning in our laws and in the minds of people; it would be a very major change and take long time to change it. We really could not retain the same meaning for these other unions. If the problem is the benefits of married people, it would be easier to change the laws. If it is a matter of respect for one's lifestyle, then changing a name will not change the respect factor. Respect cannot be gained by a name change; it cannot be bought. Respect must be earned, period. It would be better to establish another form of union like a marriage. This would end a clash of people and ideas that has been festering a long time, and if we don't do something, it will keep raging for generations to come.

Now let us look at the divorce factor in the marriage equation. Currently over 50% of all first time marriages in the US end in divorce. It is even higher for second or third marriages. We need to determine what is causing this high divorce rate and what we can do about it. It probably is not affecting the propagation of the species, but it most certainly is affecting the lives of our children.

So now the wedding is over; it was a wonderful day. All of our relatives and friends congratulated us, and we thought this union would last forever. So why do so many end in failure? There must be some reason(s) for this high divorce rate. The first thing that comes to mind is that the couple really did not get to know each other well enough. They did not adequately discuss each other's likes/dislikes, plans for the future, and their expectations. They primarily looked at their current relationship, not what is would to be like in the future. They did not discuss their preferences for number of children, how they would raise their children, their economic future, preferences/expectations, and how they would resolve differences which would occur. Also, there are the relationships with each other's friends and in–laws. These are all differences that can be very difficult to resolve if not considered before the marriage. I know there are pre-marital classes, but how well are these subjects handled? Also, it is often too late to address these issues just before the wedding. All we see then is everlasting love, trust, and confidence that we can handle any situation. This needs to be part of a Modern Living Course which should be taught in middle school and continued in high school. It should serve as a guide during the dating time.

Of course there are the changes that occur while married. These changes include the addition of children to the family, illness, accidents, deaths, and economic hardships which can all negatively affect a marriage. In the end, it is the children who suffer the most from these divorces or separations.

Some Christian churches neither recognize civil marriages nor civil divorces. As far as marriage is concerned, they maintain that a church service must be held in the church. As far as divorce is concerned, some churches do not recognize civil divorces, but some go so far as to not allow the divorced couple all the benefits of the church, Although I am sure that these churches would disagree, as they evidently do, some do provide what they called help; I see it more like punishment than help. This is at a time when divorced individuals probably need help more than ever. Some do provide a sort of divorce called annulment, where the couple's marriage is declared null and void, as if it never happened, but, we can say all day that it never happened or should have never happened, but the fact is it did happen and sometimes created children which should be a prime consideration in any divorce. In fact, the well-being of the children must always be the prime consideration in any divorce. Secondly, the well-being of the couple becomes the next consideration. Thus, forcing the parents to remain married is not always the best solution; divorce, though never a good solution, could be the only viable solution. Therefore, we can never force a person not to commit a sin including the sin of separation. It could be the lesser of two evils. So what can we do about this?

Yes, the Bible states that God hates divorce, but it seems like divorce was occasionally granted, such as the example mentioned by Moses.

Of course we can continue along the path we are now following: providing only minimal education concerning marriage and not assisting the children and parents when the marriage fails.

or

We can take a more Christian approach by teaching children about marriage before and during the mate selection process. We can support them if the marriage fails and make sure that the children are well taken care of and minimize the effects of the divorce of their parents. We must also assist the divorced couple during this difficult period and especially not punish them for their failure by shunning them in our churches. They need the assistance of the church and their friends during this difficult time. We must also have inexpensive counseling services available for married couples having problems.

RAISING OUR CHILDREN

Everybody knows how to raise children - just ask them and they will quickly assert that raising their children is solely their business and others should keep their noses out of their business. Then why do we have such a problem with so many of our children?

First of all, the world is a much more complicated place in which to grow up than it was when we grew up. It is now much more interconnected than it previously was, it seems that there is much more evil in this world, and all kids today come in contact with this evil. We are much more mobile than ever before and quickly and frequently lose track of our kids. They often have to fend for themselves. We often have to depend on others to watch out for our kids but are quick to criticize or sue them if they correct our kids, especially if they don't correct them our way or we perceive that they went too far. We have all heard that it takes a village to raise a child; well, with today's problems, it probably takes a nation to raise a child.

To try to resolve these problems, we need to go back to the beginning, back to the conception of the child. The first problem is that we have far too many children who are born without responsible parents or only one parent to take care of the child. We all know that education starts at birth, so with no parents or only one parent to provide this education, how can we succeed? Those children are already at a terrible disadvantage right from the beginning.

Somehow we must make the biological parents of children responsible for these children at least until they are 18 years old or today probably a few years older so that they can be adequately educated and/or trained. I do not believe in passing laws to force people to be moral, but we have and are proving that we cannot or will not always act morally on our own, and the children and the public suffer because of it. One of the current problems involves the idea appearing on social media that men should spread their seed as much as possible and even have a responsibility to do so. I think we could mostly eliminate this problem if we had a law which would make the father share in the financial responsibility until the child is at least eighteen years of age. We cannot continue to lose these children due to the unwillingness or inability to provide them with the education or training they need to live productive lives. Thus we must have a law that makes the parents responsible for their children until a certain age unless they are adopted, at which time the new parents take over the responsibility. If they cannot provide the necessary money to do this, the government will supply the money and those amounts will be added to the non-supporting parents bill, to be repaid to the government if and when they have some money. The only way this debt would be forgiven is when the offender dies. If we create a child, we are responsible for it …. Period! Today we can prove who the parents are, even if the mother or father lies about their part in creating this child.

Next comes a critical time in rearing the child. The first few years through the toddler stage are when children learn the most and the fastest. However, too many children are completely ignored during this time and often are left to fend for themselves. Many are not even shown love, much less taught about living during this time. Some of these young minds simply wither away. Also, during this time, some lifetime conditions show up, such as   autism, speech and language impairment, delayed motor skills, and emotional disorders.   These sorely need expert intervention at this early age to minimize the effects of the conditions. For parents desiring or needing such assistance, we must set up nurseries and preschool places to safely leave the kids during the day. This will provide a place for the children to learn to interact with their peers and learn many of the skills they need for living in modern day society. Such services must be available for all kids, not just those whose parents have the money. Costs for care should be determined on a sliding income scale, and no children should be denied care. Of course, as with most things, there are dangers associated with this. We must have checks and balances in place to ensure that we hire proper and well-trained people to man these centers, and guarantee that all of the kids get access to training.

Each state has a "Child Protection Agency" or some such agency that is supposed to be protecting our children. However, as I understand it, most, if not all of these agencies, are somehow "broken." They fail to satisfy the needs of the kids more often than help them and often make things worse. I don't know if this is due to the caliber or type of people they hire, a lack of funding, or gross mismanagement. No matter what the cause is, we must remedy this sad situation . . . . now! Some daycares and preschools are simply rip-offs, set up simply to make money. These must be shut down. They are doing more damage than good. The kids not only need better, but deserve better. Certain minimum attendance must be required unless the parents can prove they are supplying equivalent training. This could become part of the school system, but the school system itself must be cleaned up first. Not only is there a wide diversity in the effectiveness of school systems from state to state, but even within school districts. We can't add this to already inadequate school systems no matter what the reason is. We have multitudes of children receiving no training before they start school and then ending up attending sub-standard schools. We must remedy this very quickly. Many of these children are learning virtually nothing during the time they learn most quickly and easily.

Also, our Child Protection Services must be dealt with so that they can and will do their job to protect the children, which could involve removing them from the family. This includes educating the parents in child rearing, requiring it if necessary, then monitoring the family. Early on, all children must be taught what their responsibilities are if they bring a child into this world. This must start early in the grade school with teaching appropriate to the level for the age. By the time they get old enough to create children, there should be no question in their minds relevant to what their responsibilities will be.

Some of these remedies sound very harsh, but we are doing some of these things today. We take children away from their parents, but mostly do a poor job of following through with the corrective portion of it. We cannot continue to lose these children at these early formative ages.

As the children advance to the primary grades a new course of study, we will call it "Modern Living Skills," could be added to the curriculum. It would be a very inclusive class taught to all children through high school. It would cover all aspects of life, taught at the level appropriate for the age group that, the kids would encounter for much of their life. It would cover numerous areas which are now not taught at all, quickly passed over, or taught completely wrong. It would include, but not be limited to, lessons in sex, childbirth, dating, marriage, home and family economics, family life and interaction with relatives, friends, and neighbors. This, of course, would require a lot of preparation, training of instructors, and monitoring to make sure instructors are teaching what they should, rather than what they want to teach. This sounds very drastic, but we must do something to save our children. Many parents will be against this concept, and we need to leave some way for parents to provide their input, but at the same time, not to allow them to dictate the lessons. Also, parents would always have the opportunity to provide their knowledge and experience to their children.   I know parents are well-meaning, but many are limited in their ability to discipline, be good role models and openly discuss life skills. I think I had very good parents, but I don't think sex was ever mentioned; actually, many of the areas I mentioned above were never discussed. Also, many are reluctant to tell their kids to abstain from behaviors which they practiced when they were growing up or still practice, such as drug usage, sex, and smoking, using alcoholic beverages, and living beyond their means. So what can we do about this problem?

First of all, we can continue what we are doing now, namely continue to leave a portion of our children to start primary school without preparation, which often means that they missed their primary learning period and can remain behind for the rest of their life.   or

We can take a more Christian approach and make sure that all children utilize this important learning period, This means that this education must be available for all children and must be mandatory for those whose parents who cannot afford it, or who are unable or unwilling to provide it. We cannot afford to keep losing these children.

As Christians we must do everything we can to provide these children with a good life and the opportunity to better themselves.

EDUCATION DILEMMA

Since it is such an important part of our life, I hate to call it a dilemma. But unfortunately, that is exactly what it has turned out to be, a seemingly unsolvable dilemma. The first thing we should do is look at some of the problems. The first and probably one of the worst problems is we the parents: our lack of interest, our inability to recognize the need for a good education, or our lack of genuine participation in educating our children. Too many parents don't seem to realize that they created these children and therefore are responsible for teaching them how to live with the rest of humanity, how to make a living, and how they can contribute their skills and knowledge to make this a better world in which to live. This is not innate knowledge we are born with but skills and knowledge we must acquire.

The second problem is the schools themselves. In the first place, we have created very large knowledge factories. This is probably okay for many college studies, and maybe even to a certain extent for high school, but it doesn't seem okay for primary school children. They just become a number among hundreds of other children, most of whom they have never met and many of them whom they never see outside of their class. Some even get lost in the maze of hallways in the school. Of course some of these kids adjust quickly, but what about the ones that don't adjust? What I think we need is schools built to suit the needs of the students, not the wants of the politicians or taxpayers. I think small neighborhood schools would be best for small children, a place where they would recognize many of their classmates and would feel more comfortable. Their classes would be much smaller and more individualized attention could be provided. They could often walk to school or travel in a neighborhood car pool. Actually, I think we would find that to be a cheaper and a more effective alternative.   As they advance into middle school, some of these neighborhood schools could be combined but still remain fairly small.   Once the kids enter high school, they are learning to be adults and most of them could handle the larger size of the school and the large number of students. In post high school they are essentially adults, and we expect them, and they normally are able, to take care of themselves.

The next problem with schools is the expectation that one curriculum (or a single type of curriculum) fits all. So we lump many students into a large class with some devastating results. Often there are three sets of students in an average-sized class. The average students can normally absorb the material, although at a somewhat lower level, since it is presented at a level which should allow all students to absorb it. So we lose some knowledge transfer to the average students. The below normal students lose a lot of the knowledge transfer because it may be presented above their knowledge level. Many of the above average students lose much of the knowledge transfer because they soon become bored with the class and turn their minds off. By separating kids by ability, some students and most parents complain about being made a member of the dumb class, thus impeding their chance for advancement. Most parents think their child should be in the advanced class.

Then we have the problem of mainstreaming kids. We think these kids would learn better if they were included with the regular or "normal" kids. This is probably true for some, but what happens to the rest of the kids in the class? Is the teacher teaching at a lower level or more slowly to accommodate the kids being mainstreamed? What have we gained? Are we teaching these kids being mainstreamed the knowledge they will need when they finish school? Do they really need to know Shakespeare when they don't know how to balance a checkbook? Perhaps we do end up with all the kids graduating as average, but should this be our goal? To continue to keep this country the best in the world, we must educate them at their maximum level, not just average. We really need to separate these students by ability in order to train them properly. Even in high school, we should be able to, with the students' and parents' input, determine if they are college or trade school bound and train them accordingly. This determination should not be set in stone, but something that we could change course if the need arose.

Another deficiency in our school system is the problem of hiring and retaining the best teachers. There are several factors influencing this problem; including a disparity in pay between the states and even within the states. Another problem is the lack of respect for the profession. It is not viewed by the public as a very important cog in our national development. Actually, it is probably the most important component in the development and continuation of our country. Our future depends on the quality of our teachers. Thus, to survive we must elevate the importance of our teachers.

Another problem is the way we evaluate our teachers. An excessive emphasis is placed on one's longevity as a teacher, while in reality this can be a negative factor in the worth of a teacher. Teachers should improve with longevity; however, to do this they must keep current in their subject matter, in teaching methodologies and in selecting tools, to keep the students engaged. Otherwise they actually weaken in their teaching ability. Too many good teachers witness poor teachers with longevity progress up the pay scale without regard for their competency.

One of the major problems teachers have is their inability to maintain control of their classrooms. Students feel they should not be told what to do, or when they should do something. Teachers' hands are tied when it comes to methods of controlling their students and often they find themselves inappropriately influenced by the students. They don't dare touch a student, either in anger or with a good job pat on the back. Of course, teachers must have limits, but their current limits are disproportionate. The only way they often have control is with their voice, and we all know that for some kids that means nothing. Sending them to the principal's office or making them sit on the bench is also meaningless. This must be frustrating to the motivated kids who are there to learn because they get robbed of a lot of knowledge. It certainly is defeating to the teacher. The kids know what their rights are and for any infraction of their rights, real or imagined, they call their parents or even Child Protective Services. Of course this puts a lot of pressure on the teachers to explain and/or protect themselves and who will most likely end up with a black mark on their record. Is it any wonder that some teachers leave so soon after starting their teaching career? Too often it is only those who really don't care who end up staying. So what must we do? Parents must regain control over their kids, and Child Protective Services must stop interfering with the school system unless there is a true and severe case. Kids and parents must learn that while at school, the school is in control. School administrators must monitor their employees and teachers to make sure they adhere to school policy. Just like pilots are in control over their passengers, so we must also give teachers control over their students in the classroom.

Homeschooling is a right many parents demand. However, some parents abuse it and use it as an excuse for pulling their kids out of school for frivolous reasons. These include, but are not limited to, not getting along with classmates/teachers situations, which should be handled first by the counselor. They say that classes are too difficult or not appropriate, that there is too much homework, getting picked on by kids/teachers, etc. Many of these problems should be resolved in school and pulling out the kids is a cop-out not good for the kids. Also, some parents are just not good teachers, especially for their own kids. Of course, some parents provide an excellent education when home schooling their children; however, we do not find this out until it is too late to do anything about it. Kids often do not learn social skills; parents may concentrate on one subject such as spelling, science, or geography to make their own kids look good in a contest. At a minimum all home schooled kids should be required to take a state test at a testing center at the end of each year to determine if they are meeting minimum requirements.

I recently heard of a fund-raiser by the band members of a school. It was an annual event to raise money to repair instruments. Shouldn't this be part of the school budget? Are all school departments required to raise funds to maintain their department? Do the sports teams have to raise money to buy new balls, repaint the lines, and fix baskets or goals? I've heard that many of these sport teams actually make money, especially at colleges, so they don't need these fund-raisers. One reason they probably make money, is because they probably don't pay all their costs, like gym rental and repair. Shouldn't this profit go back to the school to be allocated to where it is most needed? All school activities should be treated equally.

We need to add another course curriculum which will be taught every year from first grade through high school. It would basically cover all the skills we now need to live in the modern world. We now think that these are being taught at home, but more often than not, they are not even mentioned. Students would be taught at an age appropriate level. The course would include but not be limited to sex education, creating and caring for children, raising/educating children and the responsibilities involved, dating and marriage practices and responsibilities, home economics, combined responsibilities in a family setting, career choices and selection, getting and keeping a job, and how to be well-informed responsible citizens.. These are all things that probably should be taught at home and/or church, but often few if any are even mentioned, much less adequately taught. It is showing the way our society lives and will become much more important in the future. Many parents will object very strenuously to this. The alternative is to continue to let them be educated by the media, i.e. TV, advertising, internet, and of course by their friends on the street. Do we really have a choice? For now we will call this course "Modern Living Skills."

We now find significant differences as to what is taught between states and even school districts within states. In a mobile society like we have, it is the students who suffer the most from this. When they transfer to another school or even get a job, they often are not prepared for the changes. What we need are better governmental systems guiding our educational system. Education is primarily a state responsibility; thus federal involvement should be limited to guidance of the states. This would include defining the current and future educational requirements to provide the country with the type of manpower required to maintain the standard of living we require. This would include guidance as to the educational levels we must attain. The states would be the primary authority as to what courses must be taught, the books and educational levels that must be attained and the watchdog to ensure that all students not only have the opportunity to get this knowledge within the state but also to measure that they are attaining it and monitor that there is some uniformity between the states to assist those students who transfer between states. I think this is supposed to be dealt with in the governors' conferences, but it evidently is not working. The local school districts must be responsible for providing the facilities, teaching and student materials, and teachers required for educating their students. Of course parents would be required to see that their children attend school and for supporting the educational staff. So what are we going to do? Are we going to keep doing what we are now doing, like argue who is the authority for the various facets of education, keep forcing our disjointed education down the throats of the students whether it is helpful or not? Are we going to continue to let the students, politicians, and disinterested parents define and control the classrooms?

or

Will we finally define who is responsible for the various facets of education? Will we restructure our schools and courses to provide all students with the best education possible? Will we educate parents as to what their function and responsibility is? Will we develop the "Modern Living Skills" course so that all students acquire the necessary skills to live and succeed in this complicated world? Will we develop the learning facilities so that their children can be learning during their most productive learning period? Will we teach parents and provide them the facilities so that they can provide their babies and small children with the very basic learning skills? Will we teach parents what their responsibilities are in training their children and interaction with the educational system? Wouldn't this be the Christian way of handling it?

OUR BELEAGUERED POLICE

Perhaps I could have called this chapter "our beleaguered first responders," but in this day and age, police are probably a better and more appropriate segment of first responders to discuss. However, since the police are at the forefront of the battle, I will concentrate on the police and say that this to a certain extent applies to all first responders.

We, the people, really need the police to protect us in our everyday lives. They are usually the first people we call anytime we have a serious problems. Thus we must have an undeniable close trust relationship with them. However, trust is beginning to fracture at the edges and is eroding with time. Unless we can stop this erosion of trust, we are in danger of living in or having some lawless areas within our country. This is not a good option.

Again, as with most problems, there are two sides. First, we will take a look at the law enforcement side. Too many police think they know it all and are not interested in listening to or finding out what the other side even thinks. This creates an almost insurmountable obstacle to creating a trusting relationship. Also, too many police think that force or a violent reaction will resolve the problem. They are trained in the use of force and know how to apply it effectively; too often they do just that, instead of depending on non-violent means. Thus they sometimes escalate the situation instead of de-escalating it.

 On the other side of the coin, we, the people, believe we do not have to obey or even respect police orders. We believe that we have the right to mouth-off to police, ignore their commands, and even attack them in an attempt to escape. We sincerely believe that we have the right to use any kind of subterfuge to escape our being caught and arrested.

However, we believe that police should not be allowed any use of subterfuge in upholding the law; not even a hidden camera or hiding a patrol car with a speed monitor to catch speeders. Furthermore, we expect ultra-high ethics from our police force, much higher than we expect from ourselves. Yes, we should expect a higher standard from them, but we should not and cannot expect perfection. They can and will make mistakes, and these should be remedied in a court of law, not in the street. We seem to think that justice should always be on our side and that there will be no mistakes; but we know that there have always been mistakes in administering justice and there will always be mistakes. So what is the answer?

Certainly it cannot be business as usual. This will only widen the rift between the police and us, the people they serve and protect.

or

We can take the Christion approach, i.e. we should learn to help each other, work to respect each other, get to know and interact with each other. It would be helpful to have more activities with each other and even attend classes explaining what their job is and what their expectations are.

OUR JUSTICE SYSTEM

This turns out to be one of the more difficult chapters I've chosen to write. Not only is it near and dear to my heart, but in this chapter my recommendations stray a long way from what is now our normal practice, and will also probably be contested most hotly by the citizens of this country and even the world. I know we want to punish those who wronged us or broke the laws designed to protect our citizens. I can understand this, but from my point of view, what good has it done us? We, and the world, have been punishing these lawbreakers it seems like forever, and has it really been effective? How much has it decreased crime? Are we, or do we feel any safer today than we did a hundred years or so ago? How many of those imprisoned have been reformed? How many of our resources have we used to further this punishment for crime idea? In other words, what has our payback been? Is it perhaps time we tried something else? Well, ours is considered the best justice system in the world, and I believe rightly so. Our system has many excellent points/aspects of which we can be proud. So why, with the advent of DNA testing, are we finding a fair number of death row convicts to be innocent? How could our system have found so many people guilty, whom we now know to be innocent? Technically, since they were innocent, it should have been impossible to find them guilty. There are several ways in which this could happen. First of all, a lawyer can make the jury believe that hearsay testimony is a true proven fact. It only takes a smart smooth-talking prosecution lawyer and a poor, "I could care less" defense lawyer to make the jury believe this to be true. Of course, evidence can be tampered with and be presented as factual evidence. The same problems can occur with witnesses. Their memory is usually not too good or trustworthy anyway, and when it is manipulated by the system and/or lawyers, it can become worse than helpful. Of course, the opposite is also true. How many people who have broken our laws are still free?

This points out another problem: the inequality of lawyers in our system seems to be set up to favor the more experienced and better-known lawyers over the poorer and run-of-the-mill lawyers. I believe lawyers are trained to exploit loopholes in the law, and it doesn't seem to make any difference if the loopholes are relevant or not. Actually, I think that lawyers ask for more time for investigation just to look for loopholes that could help them in their case. Truthfully our legal system is so complicated no one can really understand it.

I don't know if lawyers are taught this in law school or what; however, it seems like they truly believe their sole purpose in the court room is to win the case for their client, whether guilty or not. It goes so far as withholding evidence that could assist the other side, and they can often find legal means of withholding the evidence or just take their chances on not getting caught. They are able to get by with this too often with few or no consequences. Of course, money plays a big role in our society, and the justice system is no exception. As is always the case, the rich can hire the best lawyers and have lawyers on retention to keep them out of trouble or get them out of trouble. They can even have tax lawyers and accountants to make sure they pay as little tax as possible. Of course, poor or even middle class citizens can't afford this privilege. Yes, we do provide them with a lawyer for court cases, but would anyone care to guess the quality of these lawyers compared to those hired by the rich? Should they be able to use their wealth to do this? Actually the only purpose for lawyers in the courtroom should be to make sure justice is done, no matter if their client is innocent or guilty.

Another problem we encounter in dealing with crime is our tendency to rush to judgement. We the people need someone to blame and punish quickly. And, of course, law enforcement doesn't like open cases and even fewer want cold cases.

Corporate responsibility and the responsibility of the CEO and other senior corporate officers should be redefined. Currently we usually hold the corporate entity responsible for most actions attributed to a corporation. How can we do that? A corporation is nothing but a legally formed entity to facilitate our business practices. The corporation cannot make any decision on its own; all decisions and actions are the result of human thinking and action. So how can we hold a corporation responsible for the repercussions on the action of humans working at the corporation? Really, all this is because laws were passed to protect individuals and their assets. Admittedly, we have passed a law stating something about holding the CEO and perhaps senior management responsible if they knew or should have known about something illegal that the corporation was involved in or problems it was causing. However, I suspect the law is too vague because it seems that it has very seldom been used. Our present day multimillion and billion dollar industries, use their power and exert it on the government and society. In short, I believe we must change the law. I believe we must make the owners, boards of directors, the CEOs and/or senior management and their assets liable to malfeasance and other directives whenever they know or should have known of the improper actions by the business for which they are responsible. Of course foreign businesses would have to comply with our laws as they do now.

Another problem is our desire to be compensated for emotional suffering. Of course we get into all kinds of problems in this area. Really, what constitutes emotional suffering? How much emotional suffering must we endure and how severe must it be before we can expect compensation? Thus, lawyers work in a quagmire of laws and for some it has become an area of huge profit. Our tendency seems to be to allow anyone who can afford to sue or can find a lawyer who will take the case on commission. The size of the compensation seems to be getting larger, too. In fact, too often those who sue are awarded more money than they could earn the rest of their lives. Again, most likely the legal fees are a lot more than they should be. We seem to forget that just because we are human beings living on this earth, we will have emotional distress and/or suffering. Another problem with this kind of lawsuit is that Congress instituted these for the benefit of wronged consumers who were or are being taken advantage of by business. However, they seem to have been taken over by the large law firms. As it turns out, they seem to make most of the money and thus wronged consumers are offered a pittance return. Again, is this justice? Congress needs to change this law.

Another procedure we must change is the way our trial system works. Although it varies from state to state, in fact, it is generally the same. When we initially try someone, we not only are there to determine the person's guilt or innocence, but also determine if the person had the mental capacity to commit the crime, if the person is of the proper age to stand trial, if he has the mental capacity to understand what he did, and so on. This provides the lawyers with a plethora of reasons for skirting the guilt or innocence question. Aren't all these other items really questions concerning punishment, and do they have anything to do with the question, "Did that person commit the crime?" This is all the first trial should be determining: the guilt or innocence of the person, not if were there extenuating circumstances that could affect the punishment of the person.

Now we come to a major recommendation for changing our justice system. For centuries the world, including our country, has fined or locked up our lawbreakers, not only hoping that this stint in prison would cure them but also deter others from becoming lawbreakers. We even went so far as to execute the worst felons both as a deterrent to others and also to get them off the streets before they could repeat the crime or a similar crime. This approach simply hasn't worked! After centuries of failure, it seems that we can safely conclude that it never will work. Isn't it time to try something different? Actually, imprisonment can make crime worse because the inmates mostly just sit around idly brood about their status in life and commiserate with other inmates.

First, we need to get rid of levying a fine on lawbreakers. Too often they make a lot more money by breaking the law; thus they are rewarded for breaking the law. We must start fining them with what hurts namely: for breaking the law, they must give up all their assets and probably their family and require them to attend training classes. If they refuse to participate in the training classes, they would be locked up and still be required to attend these classes.

My first proposal is that we institute a remedial training program for all lawbreakers instead of just a jail sentence or levy a fine. This sentence of a remedial training program would not be of any definite duration, but would end when the lawbreaker is deemed cured and ready to be released back to society with no adverse record. This would remove the problem as to how long they should be incarcerated and when we should release someone from prison. They would have to be evaluated by a team of experts in the appropriate field(s). There would not be a single training program in which one-fits-all lawbreakers. Actually, there would be many training programs, such as for murder, robbery, rape, anger management, drug rehabilitation, etc. During the time period when the person would be going through this training, the government would make sure that his family is taken care of with a place to live, food, education, and whatever is necessary. This would assure that we are not punishing the innocent and distracting the lawbreaker's attention with worry about his family. Some would, of course, have to be locked up and/or restrained because they refuse treatment or are in danger of harming others or themselves. However, with time these forcing actions should decrease. Also, we would abolish the death sentence, which some states and nations already have done because death actually takes away a person's option to reform, which is not good.

When the lawbreakers are returned to society, efforts would be made to make sure that they do not return to the same environment that triggered their problems in the first place. The return to society must mandate that the person have a job enabling him to earn a living or otherwise a job would be provided for that person. The person would also be informed that while second chances are a possibility, they will be very difficult to obtain. Anything beyond a second chance would be nearly impossible.

These recommendations sound like a very expensive program, and, of course, they would not be cheap. However, some of these costs are already being incurred. For example, the costs of assisting the lawbreaker's family. . . I suspect that we are already burdening the welfare system with these costs. Training would certainly add costs, but we are already providing some training in our present system. Not all of these lawbreakers would have to be locked up in prisons so this should, in the long run, save us a huge amount of money. Of course, if this system would at all be even partially successful, we would really save money on crimes, punishment, and crime prevention. We would also be collecting money from lawbreakers which would take care of some of the costs.

We will be looked to take the lead in this area, and the world will be watching us closely. We will again be looked at by the world as the people to follow. So really, what have we got to lose?

One of the first things we must do is simplify our laws. For example, we have volumes and volumes of books just for income tax laws and regulations. Not even the tax lawyers can know all of them, much less the average citizens. It is impossible for us to know all of them. Yet we are responsible for obeying every last one of them. It is even worse with the thousands of other laws we have. In general, we have no idea what they say, much less what they mean. Our laws are primarily for the lawyers to argue about and to provide loopholes for those trying to get around or skirt the law. We are always trying to play catch-up with our laws. We try to list every possible incident which could possibly be covered by the law, and of course that is impossible. Thus, we leave loopholes for the crooked and shady. Furthermore, no language is precise enough to explain all aspects of a law; thus, we spend untold money and time trying to clarify our laws, which is impossible. We need one sentence laws, such as some religions have, from which we can judge all actions of our citizenry. We must also confiscate all of the criminals' assets so as to make sure the criminal would not gain anything by committing a crime. Also, this would help pay for their training and for supporting their family while they are in training. Finally, we would not be able to abolish locking up criminals completely. If we deem someone to be a danger to society or themselves, they must be locked up during the training period.

So what are our choices for the future?

First of all, we could keep on doing what we are now doing. We could continue to try to improve on what we have, but I don't know if we could do much in that area or if we the people would go for that. We could continue to spend vast amounts of money on a failing system and continue living in danger and fear.

or

We could try a new system of justice based on Christian values. This would try rehabilitating all lawbreakers and returning them to society. We would stop the practice of putting some of our worst felons to death. Once we put them to death, they no longer have a chance to be rehabilitated or cured. Even the worst felons deserve a chance to be rehabilitated. We could start out by instituting some of the suggested changes which I have advocated or which I am sure many others will advocate in the future.

SEGREGATION ISSUE

What happened? Supposedly we resolved the segregation problem way back in the sixties. Isn't that when we passed some laws making segregation illegal?   Why didn't that work? Why are we still fighting the problem? It is because we cannot change the hearts and minds of humans by passing a law. A law can help to change the outward behavior of humans but won't change their hearts and minds. Actually, we have seen a lot of improvement since the sixties. There are more interracial marriages, more interaction between the races, more school integration, both required and voluntary, more mixed housing developments, and more equality in the job market. Kids are playing together, and there is more interracial dating. That bodes well for the future. Of course, we still have a long way to go to make us all color-blind as far as races are concerned.   To get there we will need an internal change in the mindset of each person and only this can accomplish it. We don't want just a superficial change; we need a change of heart and mind. Because of our freedom of will, we must allot ample time for this change to fully take effect. However, we will accomplish it, but to complete this change, it will require an effort by all sides.

First of all, we must stop using the race card for all affronts, real or imagined. Second, we must stop making our demonstrations violent and directed against innocent people. Looting and burning the stores and vehicles of people who happen to be where we decide to demonstrate only increases hatred between the two sides or our neighbors who are not involved in the demonstration. We must demonstrate peacefully. We must clean up our blighted areas and slums so outside people will not be afraid to come and go through those areas. We must rid our areas of crime, especially of shootings and/or killings. We cannot live in or improve our well-being in a crime-infested area. It is not feasible for the police to take care of this problem. They can help, but the initiative and hard work must come from the people living in the area. We must begin to properly raise our children. No matter how good a mother is, it is very difficult and in these extreme conditions to do it with a single mom or a single dad. We must force these wayward dads/moms who are not supporting their biological children either emotionally or financially, to provide this support to their children. This is probably the first and most important step required to improve the well-being of people living in squalor in the slums or disadvantaged areas.

Just having the government or anyone provide the money will not get the job done. The initiative must come from inside, and only then will money assist in changing things. Even then we must all possess patience and trust that change will come. We cannot expect that overnight we can change something that has been ingrained in people for centuries, but with trust, things will change. So where do we go from here?

Of course, we can continue what we are doing now, mainly doing things and making accusations which accomplish nothing except angering the opposing side and delaying our final integration.

or

We can learn to have a little more patience and trust that we will accomplish this integration completely and in a timely manner. Meanwhile we need to get together and learn more about each other so we can accomplish our portion of this integration.

WEALTH DISPARITY

Money is the root of all evil. Is that true?   The way we desire, need, and obtain money, and what we do with the money is the cause or root of evil. How does this fit into our present day-society?

For one thing, our current philosophy seems to be that it is okay to accumulate as much money and material possessions as possible, in any way possible. Whether the ways are ethical or not seems to make no difference. Even if they are illegal, it's okay as long as we have a good chance of getting by with it, with or without the help of a good lawyer.

One of the problems with money is that the accumulation of money seems to generate a change within ourselves. It seems that the more money we have, the more we seem to need and/or desire. It seems okay to become more brazen in the ways we utilize to obtain more money. We become less concerned about the morality of how we obtain money and take more and bigger chances with using illegal means to obtain it. At some point money, it seems, takes control of our minds and our concerns are pretty much wrapped up in this endeavor; everything else seems to become secondary. This is probably what the Bible was talking about when it stated that it would be easier for a camel to pass through the eye of a needle than for a rich man to enter heaven.

This philosophy to become super rich is now producing billionaires, instead of just millionaires. It has also produced a giant disparity in the distribution of wealth within our country. It seems that today, a vast majority of our wealth, probably way over ninety percent, is controlled by a very small percentage of the very rich.

There are a couple of other problems associated with this unbalanced distribution of wealth. First of all, the concentration of wealth in a few people is reminiscent of something like the feudal system. It certainly is not the same but has some of the same characteristics. This is a recipe for a national upheaval by the poor and downtrodden against the super-rich. A second problem is that money increases the power of the rich. This power, at least at first, is felt in our government. Today these super rich are in control of corporations that are too big to allow to fail, and the government will see to it that they do not fail. They will also have undue power over the enactment of laws, which of course will benefit them and probably hurt the rest of us. It is now at a point where the only entity that can stop this trend is our federal government, and we must elect legislators who will have the guts and will to recapture control. What can we do?

We can continue to allow this trend of allowing corporations to get larger and larger. As they grow, so will their power within our government increase. There seems to be a belief within our government and with quite a few people, that this is good since in the end all of us will feel the benefits of their wealth. They don't think of the downside. Also, these super-rich are usually heavy donators to politicians.

or

We can elect representatives to Congress who will stop this erosion of the peoples' power and help us return to our Christian roots.

THE GOVERNMENT AND MONEY

The word is that the country is greased with money and runs on it. The only way this can be true is if the government is also greased with money. If this is true, we must ask, who has the money to grease the government? Certainly it isn't the poor or even the middle class. It can only be the rich, right?

A federal legislator was once asked if, with the legislators getting so much money from big business and the super-rich, does this affect his legislative decisions? The answer from one legislator (I can't remember who it was) was the classic one: "No, money has absolutely no effect on our legislative activity."   In a country that is virtually run by money, how many of us can believe this? At least once, the legislators, I believe it was the Senate or a joint House and Senate committee, investigated the money influence on the legislators.   Unfortunately, at best, very few of their recommendations were ever acted on even though some or most of those recommendations were very good.

The government is also very good at taking care of itself first. It seems like the thinking is "we will take care of you as soon as we have taken care of ourselves." They exempt themselves and/or the government from the effects of many of the laws they enact.   They enact legislature that would automatically give them an annual pay raise unless they voted to forego the pay raise. Wouldn't we all like an automatic pay raise? They also have their own health insurance program and thus do not have to be included in the health care program they legislate for the rest of us. Another item of concern is their ability to shut down the federal government by not passing a new budget bill. In this case many of the government workers will not get paid, but of course, the congressmen will continue to get their pay. How fair is this?

Another problem is the ability for one member of the Senate to keep a bill from being voted on. I'm not sure how they do this, but to give one senator the power to prevent the rest of the senators from voting on a bill is absurd. They can also do this with a filibuster. I suppose the same holds true for the House of Representatives. It is difficult to call this practice democracy. Another problem revolves around a benefit granted to our legislators that the government would pay for their defense for lawsuits. While the original intent of the benefit was probably good, it unfortunately has been used too often by too many legislators to pay for their sexual misconduct. Again I doubt that it was meant to do that, and I think it is just plain wrong.

One thing that must happen is to get rid of the entire group of lobbyists who gather around our government trying to influence not only the legislators but also the executive branch officials. I know the legislators say they need the input from these lobbyists to learn about pending legislation. However, this should be the job of their staff who can then educate the legislators they work for. I do not think the lobbyists should have any contact with our legislators or be allowed to have offices near the Capitol. The temptation on both sides is just too great.

Secondly, government officials should not be allowed to accept gifts or money from anyone, not even a single red cent. That should also be true for their families. This may sound harsh and hard to enforce, but in a country which runs on money, I believe it is absolutely necessary. Also, our entire government must come to recognize that their constituents are not there merely to provide them with tax revenues, and we the people must recognize that the government isn't there just to satisfy our needs. To accomplish this we must reduce the cost of goods and services. Otherwise, our infrastructure and services will continue to deteriorate. So what can we do?

We can continue as we have been, letting our lawmakers do what is best for them but not necessarily what is best for their constituents.

or

We can demand that our legislators work for the good of their constituents first and not for themselves. We must also severely limit their direct contacts with special-interest representatives and prohibit the money flow between them. Finally, we should demand that they must represent the nation our founders established, i.e. a Christian nation.

POLITICS AND MONEY

It seems like it is taking more and more money every election to elect new people or re-elect incumbents. The federal offices are the worst since that is where the power is and rewards are the greatest. Electing a new president is by far the most expensive. The candidates state that while some of the money comes from small donors, a large chuck comes from corporations and the rich. The money from businesses, of course, indirectly comes from the consumers, and the money from the rich most likely also indirectly comes from the consumers. This not only makes the consumers pay for all this politicking but presents us with months and months of politics, especially on TV. By the time the election is here, many individuals are so sick of politics, they often would rather not vote at all. Most importantly, these large donation are not free; these businesses and rich individuals expect something in return for their money. Of course both sides deny this, but we know that this country is run on money. So what can we do about this situation?

We can, of course, continue as we have in the past and let conditions continue to deteriorate

or

We must take all private money out of politics. A set amount of public money would be allocated to each candidate for office. A method for determining who is eligible for these funds would have to be determined. We cannot allow everyone who wants a piece of the pie to run for office just to get the funds. There would have to be strict accounting of this money by each candidate, and unused money would be returned to the government which would provide the money in the first place.

We would also make provisions for candidates to run even if they did not get selected to receive public funds. Their funds would be required to come from their own resources or donations, preferably from small donors. At any rate, that candidate would not be able to spend more money than that allocated by the government for candidates for this office. Also, unused donations would be returned to the government.

THE ECONOMY

In this country, and probably in the world, we are hell bent on getting a raise for everyone. Actually, it often means that it doesn't turn out to be much of a raise after all. As everyone's salary increases, so does the cost of producing consumer goods. A lot of this cost increase is due to increased salaries not only by the place we work, but also where we purchase our consumer products. So it is really a chain effect: as products move through the economic structure, prices actually increase at just about every point of the products' journey. Not only do we have increases due to increased cost of the product, but many overhead costs, profit margins, and taxes are often based on the current value of the product. Thus, we can end up with a vicious circle of price increases.

The end result is that not all workers receive these wage increases, or they end up with a much smaller increase because it is based on a smaller base salary. This ends up with additional people falling through the cracks. That is, more and more people can no longer afford the basics of life and end up depending on the government or other assistance sources. This again raises our cost of living, making that pay raise for some people virtually non-existent.

The solution must be a change in our mindset about salaries. Instead of demanding a raise, we need to demand a decrease in the cost of the products and services we purchase. This would be equivalent to getting a raise. Also, we would not have additional people falling below the cost of living line every year. We cannot continue with this increasing wage and cost spiral we are on without a drastic readjustment taking place in the future.

Also, our government thinks it has to assist business as much as possible. It states that it has to keep our economy growing as fast as possible in order to provide jobs and adequate salaries for all of us. This sounds good, but then why do we have to go through adjustments/recessions every so often? Something isn't quite right. Also, why is our distribution of wealth going more and more in favor of the rich? We have to ask if their economic theories really are correct.

Let us look at one area, communications, and what has happened in that sector of business. Some years ago the government decided to break up the AT&T communications conglomerate, which was becoming an industry with no or minimal competition. So what did that do? It created or allowed the creation of several smaller regional units, and each one had no or very limited competition within its area. Again, there was little or no competition, for any of these units and the consumers were left holding the bag. In this case technology did come to the partial rescue, and it created competition with cell phones and cable telephone. With internet and cell phone technology, we seem to be going through much the same scenario with cable and satellite providers in control.

To counter this loss of revenue and communication, entities had to develop new ways of gaining revenue and maintaining control. Around this time, give or take, they started making major changes to their software. This basically involved adding a lot of back door access into their systems under the guise of calling them features. This allowed people access to certain features of their software allowing them to better control their communications. These changes were certainly not added for their regular customers; in fact, we really don't have any idea what most of them are. However, likely most big businesses, charlatans, and crooks trying to cheat consumers know them well. It allows them to change phone numbers, making it virtually impossible to trace these calls. They change phone numbers to make it look like an incoming call is a local call; they make robot calls by the thousands. Of course there was the addition of the 900 numbers for which the bill for them was added to the consumers' phone bills, Yes, the phone company was the collection agent for bills of its customers who were duped by these 900 number calls. How many of these so called enhancements were good for the customer? Probably very few helped the common people. However, the government waited years to address a few of these grievances, and some they have never addressed much less resolved. When the government takes action, it is usually in the form of a fine against the corporation instead of the individuals responsible for the action. To make things worse, the fine is usually much less than the profit they have earned from the improper action. Isn't this an incentive for corporate management to behave in this way? It seems that the government is also probably controlled by these super corporations.

We seem to be developing a new business sector. All these companies want to be able to advertise that their products have been tested and recommended by certain people of specific professions. A whole set of businesses seem to be popping up who will provide these businesses with the targeted recommendations by selected people (often actors claiming to represent certain professions with which they have no association). For the most part, businesses are also allowed to test their own products or hire a company or companies to test their products. We know that tests can be designed or conducted in such a way that will produce the results they want. So if a testing company wants future business, wouldn't they make sure that the tests produce the results which the company who hired them want? This is especially harmful to us, the consumers, when testing medication and/or foods.

A favorite expression among corporate management is, "Well, it was a business decision." Perhaps some, or many, of them really believe that it is a valid excuse for doing something that hurts or cheats their customers. For them the bottom line is the most important aspect of business. So what do we do now?

Of course we can continue business as usual, maintaining that the bottom line is the most important aspect of business. We can continue adding additional people to our ever-growing poor population and adding additional wealth to the super rich. We can continue to allow the rich corporations to exert more and more control over our government and thus indirectly exert more and more control over us. Where will these policies lead us?

or

We can take a Christian approach with how we conduct business. Of course we must allow businesses and the businessmen to make a fair profit. We must also pay their employees a living wage. We cannot pay them a wage which will result in their going on welfare while some businesses get filthy rich. I know many adhere to the philosophy that if the businesses prosper, the prosperity will filter down to all. Well, it just hasn't worked that way! We must put a stop to those charlatan businesses that are out to deceive the consumers and make inferior or tainted products and selling them as first class products. We cannot continue to raise the cost of consumer goods and services, granting token raises and assume that will allow everyone to make a decent living. What we really need to do is lower the prices of goods and services instead of granting token raises. We cannot continue to create the millionaires and billionaires while too many people are living on the edge of poverty or below. While some of these super rich do use their money for the betterment of humanity, others often waste it. They say it is their money and thus they can do whatever they want to do with it. Is it really their money, or did they derive it by charging their customers too much for the product or service? Look what is happening to our drug prices. We can't make everyone rich, and we cannot afford to have a large number of people on welfare or worse. Unless we can start to lower our costs, we won't even be able to maintain our infrastructure.

MY RIGHTS

Everyone knows what their rights are, but what they don't seem to know is that other people also have rights, and at times they interfere with each other. "Well, it's my right! I know what my rights are! If you don't like it, well that's too bad; it's my right to do that. I know my vehicle is very loud, but that is the way I like it. So it woke up your baby; well, that is your problem, certainly not mine. Yes, I know that this is a quiet, residential neighborhood, but the streets are public property so I can use them as I wish. Well, good luck with getting your baby back to sleep."

One of the problems with this issue is that people keep pushing the envelope (limits) of the laws or rules of civility. They expect people to put up with more and more of this kind of behavior, a little at a time, until there are few if any limits left. Soon we are expected to accept all forms of behavior. This is certainly apparent in what has happened in the areas of drug usage, alcohol usage and associated behavior, and of course sex.

Another so called right people seem to hold dear is their imagined right to disobey the law, as long as they can get away with it and not get caught. It takes many forms, and the most popular seems to think that it is okay to disobey driving laws. Speeding and not stopping at a stop sign when the intersection looks clear seem to be the most prevalent. Some drivers don't realize that it often becomes a habit and they, after a while, don't even look to see if the intersection is clear. This causes some bad, even fatal, traffic accidents. They think it is their right to escape the police, even to the point of initiating dangerous high speed chases. The latest problem area is cell phone usage and texting while driving.

Many parents think they own their kids and thus can raise them or do whatever they want. Thus, too many parents do a very poor job raising their children and we end up with another generation of misfits. Somehow they just can't figure out that they are merely the caretakers and primary educators of the children entrusted to them, not the owners of them. Their right to do anything they wish with them as they wish is quite restricted.

Now it is the kids' turn to get lectured. They seem to know all of their rights. While in school, they have no problem in calling their parents when something doesn't go their way. Of course, the parents automatically believe their kids' version and often don't even bother to find out the other side of the story; they then raise an unwarranted commotion with the wrong person at the wrong time and place. However, they get the admiration of their child and that is what seems to count in their minds. Kids also know their legal rights and at times will call child protective services or even start divorce proceedings against their parents. Of course, children need our protection, but we should not allow them to drive the process.

We feel that we have the right to attack anyone we wish, especially on-line with our social media. We feel that we can bully others, or even print lies about them, all without any proof or sources for the information. We feel we should be able to do this without any repercussions or responsibility. We think this is an ideal medium to destroy the character and reputation of others. One thing that is becoming more and more prevalent is these innuendos, misleading statements, and outright accusations about the political leaders of both parties, all without proof or sources for their accusations. The primary reason seems to be to destroy the credibility of the person.

We are having a terrible time with our privacy issues in the communications area, especially via the computer. Hacking seems to be a daily occurrence as does using scams to fleece people out of their money. Although technology seems to offer some help, it seems it is a long way down the road with no guarantee that crooks won't keep ahead of us. Perhaps the only way to minimize this threat is to give up some of our own privacy. We must change our systems so we can trace every communication back to the originating source so that it can be put out of business. It seems that we have two choices: either put up with less privacy or continue to deal with the scammers and crooks. Well, what is the answer to this problem?

We can continue to demand and exercise what we perceive to be our rights and say the heck with other people's rights. Let's see what this gets us.

or

We can do a better job of defining our rights; i.e. we can begin to determine, if by exercising our rights, we are denying other people their rights. Rights in a society do overlap, especially perceived rights, and by exercising our rights, we may be denying others their rights. We must determine what our rights really are and how are they affecting the rights of other people? I believe the Christian thing would be to limit our own rights when they interfere with other people's rights.

RELIGION

Some people say there are five major religions, a number probably determined by how many adherents each religion has. However, there are many other religions that are not parts of these five religions. Many of the five major religions have distinct sects or variations but adhere to the same or similar precepts as the major religion.

The Christian faith is the embodiment of many sects, which all believe in the same God and the teachings of Jesus Christ. The Jewish faith and the Muslim faith also believe in the same God but differ in their belief of Jesus Christ. All three of them also adhere to the history and teaching of what is commonly called the Old Testament. Thus, all three of these major religions have a lot in common, yet they are often disagreeing and even fighting each other.

While there is a lot of agreement on some of the most basic tenets of their religions, there are some major disagreements concerning a few of their major beliefs, and there are many additional tenets concerning many of the minor tenets of their faith. If we look at them closely, most of these disagreements are really not that significant. Yet, the disagreements are firmly held and cause many heated arguments. Yes, they have even caused widespread conflicts between the factions, leading to open warfare resulting in the killing of many innocent people on both sides. History is filled with these wars precipitated by religion, even though the religions teach against the killing of people. Why would God sanction the killing of His creation for perceived differences on how to praise Him or because of differences in religious beliefs, especially minor differences? It is not only open warfare, but often in persecutions against various people. Although we can't all be correct, none of us want to admit that we could be wrong, and we refuse to compromise. When will we ever learn?

When I went off to college, I soon found out that religious discussions were quite common. I attended a freshman orientation dance and met a freshman girl. We never did discuss religion, got along great, and I walked her to her dorm after the dance. We decided that we would attend the homecoming dance together, and I dropped her off at the front door of her dorm. Everything seemed to have gone very well. A couple of days later she called me and notified me that she had found out that I was a Catholic. She then stated that she was a staunch Lutheran and therefore she could not go out with a Catholic. With that, she terminated our conversation and hung up the phone. Coming from an all-Catholic community, this was all new to me. I didn't know what to do, so I did nothing. However, we both called ourselves Christians.

We must stop calling ourselves Christians or start acting like Christians, especially in our interpersonal relations. One of the most important characteristics of a Christion is not judging our fellow human beings. That is a task that only God can do. We can judge others' deeds, but not the person who performs these deeds. That will be a major change for us, but it is a necessary change if we are to solve our problems. So what should happen now?

One of the disturbing developments in the religious arena is the destruction of public Christian icons, displays, monuments, etc. in the name of religious freedom guaranteed by our Constitution. We seem to be afraid that the sighting of these may offend some of our non-Christian friends. Does this mean that in the future our non-Christian friends must also destroy their public displays to their religion and/or that we must all tear down our churches, temples, and synagogues, because they may offend some other religion? This is not religious freedom. The freedom guaranteed by the Constitution simply means that the government will not interfere with our Christian religion, or any other religion practiced in our country, or anywhere. We should be proud of our religion and show it.

We can continue to practice our religion as we have done for centuries, which is often as a non-Christian, both in our relationship with God and our relationships with each other. We can continue to create more churches, call them Christian, and divide Christianity into more and more sects which embrace more and more non-Christian values.

or

We can start a process of defining what it really means to be a Christian and start the process of re-unifying our churches, and start living the Christian life. See section III for additional information on this topic.

WELFARE AND GENEROSITY DILEMMAS

We claim to be the most generous people on earth. We donate millions to the poor and those who suffer economic setbacks. We have donated millions for cancer research and other medical research, yet, while we have made progress in these areas, we still have a long way to go to solve these problems. Part of the problem, to a large extent, is the failure to share research results; thus, there is overlap in our research efforts. We seem to have lately resolved this problem at least partly in cancer research, but how effective it will be remains to be seen. Another problem in medical research is the amount that is actually used for studies. Too many of the funds are used for overhead expenses and for exorbitant wages to those directing the research facilities.

Now let us look at assisting the poor and those who suffer economic setbacks. First of all, we have numerous charities that assist these people. These include numerous churches and their charity branches, charitable organizations, such as the Red Cross and Salvation Army, governmental agencies, such as FEMA, and media and local requests for assistance. These cover relief efforts for almost any type of disaster, from hurricanes and tornadoes, to a family whose house just burned down or has a serious illness in the family. This involves huge sums of money, covers a host of problems, and helps a lot of suffering people.

How about our welfare programs for those who are down and out? These are the people who do not have adequate or any housing, have inadequate clothing and medical care, and don't know where there next meal will come from. This is the down-trodden segment of our population who does or must live off welfare. We do seem to have a problem with this segment of our population. It seems that we keep adding people every year but don't seem to take many off. Perhaps our increasing cost of living causes much of the problem, which causes additional people to fall through the cracks every year.

Another very serious issue is the fact that we often do not remove anyone from the welfare rolls. How can we do this when the cost of living keeps going up and we don't provide adequately paying jobs to those currently on welfare? We can't have it both ways; we either provide those on welfare with jobs and training so that they can get themselves off welfare, or we keep supporting them and their families. We cannot let them starve.

One solution is to require that everyone on welfare, who is able to work must work to help them get off welfare. As soon as they request and enroll for welfare, they would be assigned a job and training which would qualify them for a job in the marketplace. If they refuse this, they would be on their own. If they have a family and refuse to work and/or train, the family would be removed and taken care of by the government or charity. The person who refuses to work would be evaluated for physical and/or mental problems and treated accordingly. If it is determined that the person simply does not want to work, then that person, if he is not a danger to himself or society, would be on his own. He would not be allowed to have his family back unless he could work to support them.

We must also look at making our welfare and charity systems more efficient. Many of our governmental welfare systems are too bureaucratic; thus, too often they are more interested in spending additional money and hiring more people since this is normally what determines what their salary will be. The welfare administrators are also hamstrung by bureaucratic regulation and archaic procedures that severely limit their ability to help in a timely manner. Then, of course, we have the problem of unauthorized people taking advantage of welfare and getting assistance when they neither qualify nor need it. Asking them to work for it may take care of a lot of this. Also, managers must be told that they may be responsible for the welfare money they illegally distribute and/or be sent to a training camp. So what can we do?

We can continue donating to various causes with little control as to how the money is spent. We can also continue with our current welfare programs which continue to provide welfare to too many without adequate controls and increasing our welfare programs.

or

We must continue to provide for those people who cannot help themselves, but we must make it possible for many of them to become self-sufficient and get off the welfare rolls. As far as donations to various organizations, we must assure that the donations are actually going to those who need the help and not to make some of the administrators rich or funds for unnecessary administrative costs.

FOREIGN AID

The United States is the leader in foreign aid to countries around the world. I believe we have sent more assistance to other countries than any other country in the world; in fact, perhaps more than all the other countries combined. Unfortunately, some of this aid had strings attached, as did much of the assistance sent by other countries. Also, some of the assistance was wasted because we did not or could not get it to the people who really needed it; instead it ended up in the hands of local profiteers who used it to enrich themselves and increase their power. Of course, some of these foreign aid programs seem to have been very successful. This would include the Marshall Plan for rebuilding Europe after WWII, providing Yugoslavia with a field hospital after the earthquake in Skopje after their devastating earthquake, and other cases of foreign aid. What can we do to improve our assistance to the rest of the world?

We can continue to provide assistance as we do now, which ends up wasting a lot of money, that often ends up in the wrong hands.

or

What I propose is a para-military organization intimately connected with all the branches of our military. This organization would be able to draw on the military to provide it with the equipment, personnel, intelligence, transportation, and anything they require to accomplish their mission. Their mission would be to respond to worldwide requests for assistance with disasters.

The US military is the only organization in the world which has the organizational structure, access to worldwide bases, trained personnel, equipment, and the ability to accomplish this mission. The only reason for the paramilitary branch would be to remove the stigma foreign countries would have to the US military being in their territory. They would coordinate the help required from the various military branches.

It would be a fast reaction force ready to depart for the disaster location within hours and to coordinate with the national and local governments for enough control to accomplish the mission as efficiently as possible. There may be some resistance from foreign governments at first, but once they would see that it is simply a means to provide a speedy relief project, they would accept it. While we seem to be the biggest donors in these situations anyway, we would probably have to set up something with the United Nations to accept donations from other countries and funnel them to the relief effort.

GUN CONTROL

This is another area causing extreme controversy and public division in our country. It is the fodder for much discussion and opinions from the local taverns to the halls of Congress. It has probably been with us since we approved and adopted the Constitution; however, it seems to have become more intense in the last fifty years or so. The main point of contention seems to be the question as to whether our Constitution allows us to bear arms, not whether it is a good idea to do so. To those who believe that the Constitution guarantees us the right to bear arms, the question as to whether it is a good idea to do so is a moot point, not worthy of discussion. To those who believe the Constitution does not guarantee citizens the right to bear arms, the question as to whether we should allow people to bear arms is the only point worth discussing.

In reality, the question of bearing arms is really an ethical question, not a legal question. That does not mean that we can't pass laws to control the sale and use of guns. However, the opponents of gun control are hesitant to go along with any control since they are afraid that it would be the beginning of eventual total gun control. However, if those who are in favor of gun control could agree that the Constitution guarantees us the right to bear arms, it should take care of this fear. Maybe that could become the basis of a compromise between the two sides and open the doors to a compromise method of providing some control to keep dangerous people among us from acquiring guns. In the meantime, the disagreement is tearing our country apart. So now what?

With the latest school shootings, we again have many people who want the teachers armed to protect the children. The

Bible states or insinuates in several places that "violence begets violence." Yet many Bible-reading people who often quote the Bible are advocating arming the teachers to solve the problem of school shootings. It just goes to show that we select what we want from the Bible and disregard what we don't want to believe. Really, we can't have it both ways. So what if we do arm the teachers? First of all, teachers are human beings, and thus they will make mistakes. We cannot predetermine what these mistakes will be, but the thought of what these mistake could be, frightens me. Secondly we will have at least a generation of kids who are literally or figuratively educated at the point of a gun and taught that the way to fight and/or resolve violence is with violence or the threat of violence. Will this decrease violence in the future?

We can continue to argue this seemingly unsolvable problem forever, while more and more people who should not own guns obtain them and unfortunately continue to use them to kill innocent people. This includes people who obtain guns legally but should not have been able to obtain them legally; this is one of our biggest problems. It is true: guns themselves do not kill people, but people who obtain and use these guns do kill people. So does it make any difference as to who or what killed the children? Either way they are dead.

or

We could state that most people may own guns. However, we must make sure that certain people will not be able to own guns and obtain and use these guns to kill people. We must make sure that mentally ill people and people who are prone to force everyone to adhere to their warped ideas should not able to own guns. We must establish an automated national registry of people who are not allowed to own guns and have enforceable laws to prevent their buying of a gun. We must also be able to use this registry to find people who are stockpiling weapons and ammunition. We should be able to track every gun. All gun owners should also be trained in the use of the guns. How many people must we allow to be killed before we do anything about it?

First of all, I would support the right to own guns, but I cannot in good conscience support the right of anyone to own these guns specifically developed for the military and can and do kill many people at once. Nobody needs to own these weapons, especially terrorists and mentally ill kids and adults. They can also obtain these weapons by stealing them from legal owners. In our country that is just asking for trouble. Neither can we arrest and/or treat the mentally ill people fast enough. We are finding mentally ill people faster than we can take care of them. The question is, why do we have so many mentally ill citizens? Basically, we have a very violent-oriented society. What causes us to breed this violence? I do not think there is a single cause for this; it is a combination of factors. We must determine the causes for this and correct them. First of all, the fetus, during gestation, is exposed to many chemicals and additives. Many are also exposed to various drugs and alcohol while they are developing, mainly by the mother, but current research indicates that the fathers' habits can also affect the sperm and in turn affect the fetus. As far as I know, we do not know what the long term effect this has on the babies as they grow up. As the babies grow up, they are exposed to many more chemicals and additives via the foul air they breathe via pollution. Again we do not know what the long term effects this has on our growing children. We must determine this and institute corrective action.

DEMONSTRATIONS

One of the most revered and treasured of our freedoms is our right to demonstrate. It is used to express our feelings toward or against some thing or some action. Done in the right way, demonstrations can be and have been a powerful tool used to protect our freedoms. This right has been used since before the Revolutionary War.

However, the way we use this freedom is now threatening our right to use it. It is becoming ever more violent and affecting innocent people, who are getting injured and occasionally even killed. Often property is damaged or destroyed. Is there any recourse against the demonstrators? Even more ominous is the fact that some of the demonstrators could care less about what they are demonstrating for or against. They are often merely people paid to show up to protest and are often the very ones who instigate the violence and damage. In many cases, once the demonstration is over, protesters leave behind a terrible mess that is very expensive to clean up and someone else, usually the taxpayers, must pay the clean-up costs. We must find a way to stop the violence and property damage during a demonstration and a way to make the demonstrators responsible for the cost associated with their demonstrations. The general population is getting very tired of paying for all these costs associated with demonstrations. What can we do about this? We can continue to allow these protestors to act in whatever way they wish and continue to suffer the consequences.   or

We must find a way to hold them responsible for their illegal acts, make them pay for the repair and damage they do, and to bear the costs of cleanup after the demonstrations are over.

LIFESTYLE

How do we live? How we live affects our thinking, and thus how we act. Which comes first and what is the result of this? Basically it is the chicken vs. the egg paradox. Do we consider ourselves the center of the universe and the rest of the people as a resource we can and do use for our purpose? Or do we merely view others as something to ignore unless they get in our way? In that case we push them aside so that we can go forward with our own agenda. Thus, we really don't care what their needs are or what they think. Certainly not everyone is like this, but we seem to have reached a threshold number of people who think that way. So how are people behaving in these circumstances?

First of all, let's look at our driving habits since they seem to be a good indicator of a person's mental attitude. How many people bother to actually stop at a stop sign? How many people pay little or no attention to speed limits? Are they careful to watch for pedestrians or school buses stopped for loading/unloading school children? How many pull out in front of a vehicle at an intersection even though the path is clear behind that car? Do they depend on the other driver to slow down to prevent an accident? And so it goes on and on. It seems many have the attitude that the road was built for them, and everyone else should get out of their way. Drivers are also becoming mean, such as cyclists surrounding a car on the interstate and then damaging the car and/or injuring the driver. The police are often afraid to chase them fearing that they will become the next victim. Doesn't this sound like lawlessness?

How many people think that the government has no right to tell them to adhere to safety measures? Examples would be wearing safety belts, wearing helmets, slowing down for icy or dangerous situations, and not texting while driving. Their argument is that they are the ones that will get hurt and that is their right to decide. First of all, there are often others who get hurt or even killed. Secondly, who pays when they get hurt? They may claim that their insurance will pay. In reality, insurance often does not cover the entire cost, and it raises the cost of insurance for everyone. Additionally, can any amount of payment replace a lost life? Thus, we all pay in some way or the other.

Another characteristic of the current generation is their affinity or addiction to danger. Not only do they drive dangerously, but they also court danger in many aspects of life. They seem to need extremes in their life, such as extreme sports. They not only love to watch and witness them, they often participate in extreme sports. They seem to disregard danger and evidently think that they can avoid injury and not be subject to death. They love to party and celebrate with exuberance. They find any excuse for having a party or celebrations and celebrate to extremes. They love to get passed out drunk and/or high on alcohol and drugs. These parties and celebrations are often accompanied with wild sex, some of which may be unnatural/unlawful. Although this is not new behavior, it does seem to be increasingly more common and extreme.

Another problem plaguing us is our addiction to sex. We are bombarded with sex or allusions to sex constantly. It is rife in our social media, TV programming, the movies, games, advertising, and just about anything with which we come into contact. Businesses use sex to advertise and sell their products. The way we dress and act is often suggestive of sex. It is very pervasive and with us all the time. The sex drive is very strong, as it has to be, since it is the way we assure the continuance of the human species. However, it also can be the downfall of many people. We seem to have so many cases of rape, child molestation, and other sex crimes nowadays. I really don't think it is due to more accurate reporting but more probably due to our obsession with sex. Unfortunately, we are all different in our sexuality, and for certain people who have a strong and/or perverted sexuality, the constant barrage of sex in our media drives them over the edge. Many people would say that they have no responsibility for these people, but as Christians we have a responsibility for all of our fellow human beings. Can we continue to maintain our obsession with sex?

Another common behavior is the way we adorn ourselves. Long hair, especially with girls, is now in vogue again; however, all types of hair styles are okay, along with dyeing the hair any color, especially bright colors which some favor. Using two or many colors in the hair in streaks or any way is also in style. Men may have anything from long hair to shaved heads and are also starting to use more color. Having copious facial hair is also very popular again. As far as dressing goes, it seems like weird clothes are also making a comeback. Another popular fad is to have tattoos. The larger and more colorful they are, the better as long as they are noticeable. While these forms of expression are not necessarily bad or even distasteful, it all depends on why they are done. Is it because people are dissatisfied with the way they are, or is it primarily an attention getter?

People also "just want to have fun." This is fine except that they want this without working to earn it or at least by working as little as possible. Also, they don't want anyone putting on restrictions as to what they can do or where they can do it. They don't seem to have any problem in using other people against their will to have their fun. Unfortunately, they often trash the place of their gathering and then depart, leaving the owner to clean up and pay for damages.

Everyone wants his/her five minutes of fame and recognition and seems willing to go to some extremes to get it. This includes performing illegal or outrageous acts or pretending to perform them and then making videos of them and posting them on internet.

Another problem involves our need to assist those who become addicted to these behaviors. We now have programs for those who have become addicted to alcohol, drugs, gambling, and so forth. We spend enormous amounts of money and effort to help and cure these people. While we do have some success in these areas, we are a long way from eradicating these problems.

Most recently the breaking news, was another terrible school shooting. The shooter was a former student who was expelled for behavior problems, and most likely the shooting was probably a cry for help from that student. In any case, he should have received help, but what happened? He was probably expelled and set free to do whatever he wanted to do. He should have received mental care, even against his will, until he was cured. I know people will say that it is his right not to be forced to receive mental care, but what about the rights of all these students who were injured and/or killed? Don't they have the right to be safe in their school? Yes, we will make mistakes by committing him for mental care, but we also made a mistake by freeing him. Which mistake is worse? We must make sure this does not continue to happen.

Again, in all of these areas, we must act in moderation and always first determine how they affect other people and change our behavior accordingly. So what is the answer?

Of course we can always do nothing and continue to live the way we are now living. Therefore, nothing would change, and we would continue living as we are living today.

or

We could change our style of living, and if we changed it adequately, we could see a vast improvement in our lives. Our major change would involve our outlook on our environment and our fellow human beings. We would no longer see ourselves as the central figure in our relationships with our fellow human beings, but would always consider other people's feelings and needs. This change alone would result in a vast change in the conditions in our world. We would be living the Christian life and enjoying all the benefits we derive from this life style. This is the crux of the change we must make if we are going to resolve our present day problems.

SUICIDE

Suicide! We don't even want to think about it. Just to mention the term makes a person tremble. Suicide is so foreign an idea for us, we cannot even comprehend the term, much less the action. Some religions have even stated that if anyone commits suicide, they will surely go to hell. And some of them will even deny victims a church burial service. We will take a closer look at this later, but first let us take a look as to why people commit suicide.

So what causes people to commit suicide? This is hard to determine since there are a number of factors coming into play, and they cannot be easily separated. One important factor is the mental state of the individual. There are several, perhaps many, mental conditions which can come into play when suicide is contemplated or accomplished. However, we cannot really determine this until it is too late. Thus they are usually left to fight this condition on their own. Drug usage, especially the ingestion of narcotic or psychedelic drugs without a doctor's prescription and monitoring by a doctor, also greatly reduce a person's ability to fight suicidal urges and the ability to think clearly. Of course, the usage of alcoholic beverages, because of their widespread usage, is probably an even greater factor in suicide cases.

A second factor is the inability of a people to handle and resolve several problems plaguing them. They realize that they must resolve these problems if they are to continue leading a productive life. Their ability to resolve these problems is often, or probably usually compromised by their mental problems as well as eroding self-esteem, a background of living with a lot of criticism, an attitude of feeling pushed into a corner with no way out --- all can lead victims to the conclusion that the only solution to these problems is suicide.   They have become incapable of satisfactorily solving   these problems and eventually they come to believe that suicide is the only way to resolve these problems and that they are making the correct decision for all those involved. Eventually they see it as the only viable solution.

Now let us look at the attitudes about suicide. First of all, we all tend to shun anything to do with suicide. Thus, people avoid telling anyone of suicidal thoughts or a potential suicide attempt and therefore no one is available to help them. The suicide hot line of course is a big help if they can get involved, but too often they are not contacted or contacted too late. They usually, or at least often, are left to battle it alone.   So what can we do?

First of all, we can continue to avoid the problem, or pretend that it doesn't exist. Of course, then nothing will change.

or

We can change society's attitude about suicide and admit that it really is a mental illness, not a character weakness. We can attempt to improve our diagnostic ability to identify this illness sooner and provide the needed assistance. With the change in society's attitude toward suicide, it will encourage people thinking about suicide to come forth and get assistance before it is too late.

The World Order

After the two world wars, the victors of the wars and the other powerful nations set out to establish a world order that would make sure that these world wars would not be repeated and world peace would be assured. After the first war, they established the League of Nations, which was to be a sounding board for nations to settle their differences without going to war. After the second war, they established the United Nations, which essentially had the same mission. Regrettably, the League of Nations failed within a short time. The United Nations, which was established after the Second World War is still functioning, but its effectiveness is certainly questionable.

After both wars, the world powers also set about to change the geopolitical structure of the world. Territory was taken away from some countries and added to other countries or formed into new countries. Too often this was done without regard to the desires of the affected people. Other areas had such a mix of ethnicities that there was certainly no way of satisfying the desires of the people affected. Old alliances were often destroyed and new ones were formed. Some are still viable, but others have disappeared. Europe, the center of the last two world wars, plus a long history of war among the countries of Europe, finally decided to form a politically united Europe. This was to entwine the countries of Europe economically, politically, and culturally to such an extent that it would be difficult if not impossible for them to wage war against each other. The same was done, or rather forced upon the Balkan countries of south central Europe. The result was a forced combination of several different ethnic peoples with different religions, lifestyles, and economic expectations. It was probably preordained to fail, and of course it did. Now we have many countries, after several wars, in what was formerly Yugoslavia. Other countries such as Czechoslovakia simply divided into two countries. As the Cold War heated up, the West created the NATO alliance to counter the eastern threat from the USSR. The USSR in turn formed an Eastern Europe alliance to counter the NATO threat. Meanwhile, in the US, a unique ethnic problem had developed from our practice of settling the Native Americans on reservations after we defeated them. Of course, this helped them to retain their unique cultural heritage, but at the same time made it very difficult for them to participate in the development of the United States. Of course there are ethnic peoples all over the world who are trying to become their own country which could lead to war. Africa and the Middle East are political messes which have simmering or active wars going on all the time, Weapons development has progressed immensely since the last world war and now includes nuclear weapons, missiles, submarines, and bombers to deliver them. These weapons are now ending up in smaller nations who have unreliable leaders who think they can win their battles with the threat of nuclear weapons. The world has now acquired the capability to destroy itself. Countries also developed all kinds of trade agreements which would tie the world together and thus decrease the likelihood of another major war. They seemed to have all the bases covered to make this a peaceful and prosperous world in which to live. So what is happening?

Things just haven't worked out the way the builders of our geopolitical system envisioned or hoped. Basically they didn't include the most important factor (human nature) in their plans and/or visions. They also forgot that they could not control the natural forces of nature. It is these factors that have brought us to the difficult position we are now confronting. It may not seem too bad or unmanageable now, but we are just beginning to confront the problems facing us.

First, let us look at the problems which human nature is presenting. This geopolitical system was established primarily by the rich and powerful segments of the world population. Thus they simply didn't understand the problems or desires of the remainder of the population or didn't take the time to try to understand. Not only were they poor and the workers who kept our economic engine running, they were afraid that nothing would change. The wealth would not trickle down, as promised, so they would always remain the poor workers who kept the economic engine purring along. Travel and communications have been developed to the point where even more people could find out how the rest of the world lives and how their living standards compare to the rest of the world. They know how the rest of the world lives and where they want to be. One way or other, that is just where they end up. War, poverty, and natural disasters are driving many of these people to move in massive numbers to other locations, often in other countries. How can we stop them when we know that returning them will mean death? As conditions in the world worsen, the number of migrants will increase greatly, and countries won't be able to afford to return them, even if they wanted to. Climate change could cause this migration to increase by millions. How will we be able to handle it? A lot of people will also be affected by trade restrictions and disruptions/wars caused by ethnic groups fighting for their ethnic rights/wants. There are a lot or reasons why the movement of people will continue and increase in the coming years, so we had better be prepared.

The League of Nations died a long time ago, and the United Nations is having its own problems. Political alliances are changing or not working too well. Trade agreements are being questioned. More and more ethnic groups within existing countries are seeking some sort of limited independence or even complete independence. Our entire geopolitical structure is in danger of collapsing. Even our beloved democracy which we thought would spread worldwide is faltering. The entire world did not embrace democracy, and even where they did accept it, they usually built a modified version of the democracy we know. So what can we do?

Of course, we can continue as we now are, and let the world continue to on its merry way.

or

We can meet these changes and dangers head-on and create change where necessary.

We need to create an international geopolitical system that to a greater or lesser degree satisfies all people. Our current system creates countries, political systems, and economic systems that primarily satisfy one group of people in each country, and we expect or force all others to accept it. Even in the melting pot of the world, namely the United States, we have problems integrating all these groups of people into one group with one system. The answer is not creating a separate country for each group; this would create a whole new set of problems. Perhaps groups of semi-autonomous states within a country would be a step in the right direction, all under the overall control by a central government formed by these semi-autonomous states. Creating such a structure would certainly require a lot of thought and work. To create some equity between countries would also be difficult but would have to be done. Perhaps we would also need an overriding political entity to oversee the world structure and resolve differences, at least until we learned to all live with each other. Of course, we would probably have to have some trade agreements until things got settled and evened out.

Another problem we would have is the current concentration of power and wealth distribution in the world. The current geopolitical structure made sure that those who currently are on top as far as wealth and power is concerned would retain their lead in wealth and power. Think of what would happen if we continue this concentration of power and wealth. What we really need to do is use our wealth and power to educate and provide the poor to become more equal to the wealthy and powerful people. Basically, we would need to help the poor people help themselves. Just handing a people wealth and power has never worked.

Realistically, the only way this can work is by initiating a change in ourselves; to accomplish this we must become "a kinder, gentler people." Only then can the plan be successful.

SUMMARY AND RECOMMENDATIONS

It seems that in many ways we are an angry, frustrated, argumentative, and stubborn people. If things don't go our way, we are quick to fly into an angry rage and use violence in an attempt to resolve the problem. We see this anger and frustration popping up all over. Domestic violence seems to be rampart, road rage is everywhere, bar fights seem to be a regular occurrence, and even fights in schools and sporting events occur too often. A lot of this anger is the result of frustration and arguments. Somewhere along the way we never learned to be patient and understanding with our fellow people.

Perhaps we learn about this violence as a means of resolving our problems from the video games we play and from so many of the TV shows and movies we watch. It seems that many of them feature violence as the only or best means of resolving problems. Another factor is the availability of guns and other weapons which all too often we end up using to resolve a problem.

So why do we have all this anger and frustration in us? Part of the problem is that we never learned how to handle failure. We always expect to win. That is how we grew up as children. Secondly, our expectations are too high and unrealistic, and when we cannot realize our expectations, we become angry.

We need to resolve these stressors to reduce the tensions which frustrate us and make us angry. The solutions must be reasonable, logical, and Christian. We are, after all, a Christian nation; at least we call ourselves a Christian nation.

So, should we not live as Christians or stop calling ourselves Christians?

Some of the aforementioned recommendations may seem to be far-out and outside the box. However, I believe we must implement this type of solutions since our problems are quite severe and require new ways of viewing and resolving them. As far as my recommendations are concerned, I tried to make sure that they simplified things and that they are solutions that consider solid values and each individual's worth.

We certainly cannot attempt to implement all of these recommendations at once. We need to prioritize them and make long range plans to execute them. Some of them will require a lot of preliminary planning by experts in the field, the passage of new laws, and a lot of training to implement them. This would be the case with our justice system. In the education area we should start by implementing the training for the pre-school children. We will have to do this planning and development for each of the areas. We will also have to train experts for each of the areas. This will all take time, but in the end it will be well worth the effort and expense. So where do we go from here?

I have introduced some very tough solutions for some problems, minor solutions for other problems, actually no solutions for other problems, and many problems I have not even discussed. However, the bottom line for these and most other problems, is one overriding solution which we must implement; otherwise suggested solutions and most other solutions will be of minimal help or no help in resolving these problems. This solution involves a change of heart for all of us. This involves "Thou shalt love the Lord thy God with all thy heart, and with all thy soul, and with all thy mind. This is the first and great commandment. And the second is like unto it, Thou shalt love thy neighbor as thyself." This way we will become "a kinder gentler person/people." We will then have accomplished the next great advance of mankind.

Most likely in the near future many people will resist all these changes and think that we can continue just as we are now and everything will work out fine. However, in time, I believe conditions in this world will get bad enough so that more and more people will see the merit of making some major changes. Should we wait that long?

or

We can get started discussing these changes, or alternative changes, that we can develop. This would give us a head start delaying or preventing some of the hard times we could suffer if we don't make any changes.

SECTION II

THE PHYSICAL UNIVERSE

INTRODUCTION

This seems to be a good place to address the creation of man and the development of the human race after creation, because it did occur in our physical world.

I also want to touch on the status of the science of the world we live in. It has been a roller coaster of knowledge about the universe and so called setbacks letting us know how little we really know.

TABLE OF CONTENTS

THE CREATION

Genesis - Good News Translation (GNT)

The Story of Creation

Genesis 1:1:

"In the beginning, when God created the universe, the earth was formless and desolate."

Scientific version:

About 13.8 billion years ago a small glob of very densely packed energy and/or matter exploded and expanded very rapidly. This is called the Big Bang. Thus the universe was created.

Genesis 1:3-5:

"Then God commanded, 'Let there be light'—and light appeared. God was pleased with what He saw. Then He separated the light from the darkness, and he named the light Day and the darkness Night."

Scientific version:

About 380,000 years after the Big Bang, the universe cooled off enough to allow light to glow, and then there was light.

Genesis 1.6-8:

"Then God commanded, 'Let there be a dome to divide the water and to keep it in two separate places'—and it was done. So God made a dome, and it separated the water under it from the water above it. He named the dome Sky.”

I interpret this to include all the things that had to be established to make the planet habitable. What this includes is detailed in the next paragraph.

Scientific version:

After the earth was formed, it was not habitable. Water had to be established on the earth, and much of that water was probably brought to earth by meteors and comets. The water had to be separated into oceans and lakes with a good amount in the skies to provide fresh water. The earth had to be positioned the correct distance from the sun and at the correct angle rotation and angle of inclination.   The atmosphere had to be established with the correct mixture of gases, especially oxygen and carbon dioxide. The earth itself had to have the correct mixture of minerals. All this plus much, much more had to be done before the earth could support life. Scientifically all this was happening while God was making the planet habitable.

Genesis 1:9-10:

“Then God commanded, ‘Let the water below the sky come together in one place, so that the land will appear’—and it was done. He named the land Earth, and the water which had come together he named Sea.”

Scientific version:

Next the continents rose out of the sea and the water was gathered into basins, which we call oceans.

Genesis 1:11-12:

"Then He commanded, 'Let the earth produce all kinds of plants, those that bear grain and those that bear fruit—and it was done.'[12] So the earth produced all kinds of plants."

Scientific version:

Once the earth was habitable, plants of all kinds developed and grew, covering much of the earth. Life had now established itself on the earth.

Genesis 1.20-21:

"Then God commanded, 'Let the water be filled with many kinds of living beings, and let the air be filled with birds.' [21] So God created the great sea monsters, all kinds of creatures that live in the water, and all kinds of birds."

Scientific version:

When the plants established themselves, other forms of life began to appear. It is difficult to determine just when they began to appear in relation to plants. It could be in the same time frame, depending on what one considers to be animal life. Bacteria and other single-celled creatures developed much earlier than did the birds and fish. So when this all happened is open to question.

Genesis 1:24-25:

"Then God commanded, 'Let the earth produce all kinds of animal life: domestic and wild, large and small'—and it was done. So God made them all, and He was pleased with what He saw."

Scientific version:

Once the single-celled creatures were alive, they continued to develop into more sophisticated creatures and after many years, we had the animal life to inhabit the world.

Genesis 1:26-2:

"Then God said, 'And now we will make human beings; they will be like us and resemble us. They will have power over the fish, the birds, and all animals, domestic and wild, large and small.' So God created human beings, making them to be like Himself. He created them male and female."

Genesis *2:7* :

"And the LORD God formed man of the dust of the ground, and breathed into his nostrils the breath of life; and man became a living soul."

Scientific version:

The major question would be, "When were Adam and Eve living on this earth?" Biblical scholars seem to indicate that they first inhabited the earth somewhere between 6000 and 12,000 years ago.

It appears that the scientific and Bible versions are not that different except for the timing of the events. This does not quite agree with current scientific thought. Science teaches that human-like beings started evolving at least 100,000 to 200,000 years ago, but the most likely time when they really looked like and acted/lived like humans may have been about 10,000 years or so ago. Again, these figures vary greatly depending on who studied which aspect of Homo Sapiens. Anyway, the rate of evolution was accelerated at this time, so I would select this time as being closest to the actual time period. So sometime after 10,000 years ago, we probably had humans who were anatomically similar or the same as present-day human beings. Since the whole race would not necessarily experience all change the same way at the same time, it leaves open that the major changes could have occurred in only one man or man and woman. It leaves open the possibility that there was an Adam and Eve which were present about 6,000-10,000 years ago, and it was their offspring who eventually populated the whole world. That leaves open the question as to what happened to the remaining population. It seems that the scientific and Bible versions are not that different except for the timing of the events.

In my opinion, man does not become a human being until the spirit component enters the physical body. Exactly when that happened, we will probably never know. I would surmise that it probably happened in the 10,000 years ago period, since much of our evolution had occurred by then. However, we are all guessing. Further messing up our guesses/estimations as to when we became human is in trying to explain certain facts that occurred before that time. This is primarily a problem on the scientific side. For the religion scholars, the primary problem seems to be in establishing some of the truths on the remainder of the Bible which refer back to Genesis. Thus, we seem to have an unsolvable problem.

Another problem is the transference of the changes that have taken place in humans throughout the centuries/millennium. What happened to the relatives of the human beings whose branches died out is not important. However, what happened to the branch that became us and the branches that interbred with those beings is important. On the scientific side, we would have to assume that those changes happened to everyone or were transferred by natural selection to all others. Many of these could have occurred before the migrations out of Africa. On the Bible side, we would have to assume that they occurred early in the dispersion of humans, and that the dispersion of people was mainly by descendants of Adam and Eve. This could be explained if we assume that the Numbers book of the Old Testament contained only the history of people in a part of the Middle East.

This battle between the church and science has been going on for almost forever. Traditionally I think science has generally come out the winner, and I don't think it will be any different this time. It is very difficult to win any battle with science, especially since science is a product of God, and He was and is a very logical being. Thus, if He created the logical means of developing human beings, why would He use supernatural means instead of the logical means which He had already developed? We just need to determine how He did this. First of all, a man/woman does not become a human being until it is combined with a spirit being. Thus, the humanoid beings could have been residents on earth for millions of years before He combined them with a spirit being which would have turned them into a bona-fide human being. Who knows what happened to all the non-Adam lineages; they could have died out like many lineages did back then. Also, was there only one Adam? There could have been many of them, but the Bible only kept track of the one lineage that led to Christ. Also, I believe that all these population estimates used some invalid criteria in their estimating. I don't think they really had correct birth and death estimates, and they had no basis for estimating losses due to wars, disease, or just plain lineage terminations. So I cannot place any faith in any of these estimates.

Questions that arise then beg the further question: what difference does it make as to what theory we accept to believe? We have been living with this disagreement for more than a thousand years, we have not resolved it, and probably never will, we are still living well even with our disagreement and will be able to continue to live well with either theory. The problem really is the fact that we human beings love to disagree and argue and just hope that eventually we will be proven correct. In reality it will not make any difference who, if anyone, is proven correct. So why not call a truce and just agree to disagree?

THE DEVELOPMENT OF THE HUMAN RACE

Human beings continued and are continuing to evolve by normal evolution; at first by intermarrying with other humanoids such as the Neanderthals, until they died out. However, there were some major changes in their lives that increased the rate of this evolving, mostly in how their minds worked and in how they lived. Several of these occurred before there was any written language. Thus, we have no record of these changes including the following major changes that really affected mankind but for which there are no records.

The first of these would be when our ancestors started walking on their two legs, rather than on four. This must have been a very major change that affected not only how they thought, but also how and where they lived. The second change for which we have no record would be when male and female entered into monogamous relationships. They picked their spouses for life, and again this must have changed not only how they thought, but certainly how they lived. There is no record as to when they occurred. However, we know they did occur and are still part of our human culture today. Another major change that occurred mostly before written records were kept is the domestication of animals and the beginning of farming. Among other changes, this changed the people from being primarily nomadic to settling down in one place and starting to build cities.

There have also been several major changes since written records have been kept. We know more about these changes and how they affected the people. The first one was the introduction of large scale religions. Of course the Jewish faith was already strongly entrenched in the Hebrew culture, which at that time was a relatively small group of people. There likely were several other small religions and probably some large ones already flourishing. What brought the major change was the rise of the Christian and Islam religions and the widespread migration to other parts of the world. Thus, the accelerated changes in people affected a large part of the known world. There were major upheavals during that change and for a long time after the change. There were the crusades, the Spanish Inquisition, the Reformation, and many killings. It was a truly unsettled time.

The next major change that accelerated the development of the people at large was the Enlightenment and Discovery era. It was during this period that the people of the world expanded their minds greatly. This included the arts, writing, painting, music, philosophy, geography as well as all of the sciences, medicine, geology, psychology, chemistry, physics, and learning in every field. It also included the discovery, settling, and exploration of far-away lands. It was indeed a time for mankind to greatly expand their minds. It was a time of great activity and led directly to the Industrial Revolution. Some consider the Industrial Revolution as a separate major advancer of the human intellect, but I have included it with the Enlightenment and Discovery Period.

So what comes after that major change which expanded our minds considerably? I consider us to be in the middle of another major change. Some call it the atomic age; others call it the information age. Perhaps it is both, but I believe they are just the forerunner of an even more major change. We are being prepared for the change that will not only expand our minds, but also our hearts. It will change the way we view life itself. The atomic era makes us fear a nuclear war, which could end life on this planet as we know it. The information era provides us with virtual instant access to all information and contact with all other humans. It also threatens to take away our beloved privacy and open our lives to everyone. That is almost as frightening as atomic warfare. Between the two, we will be forced to rethink the purpose of our life here on earth and how we live it. That sentence is the crux of the major change which I believe we are now involved in. While we will be called upon to lead this change, the whole world will have to participate in this change. Thus, we are entering a major change in how we live and act, and this change is preceded by and accompanied by major upheavals, including warfare just like all the other major changes in human living and thinking were. I certainly do not see this as the end of our civilization, as some people do, but as a change for the better in the future. I am confident that we will accomplish this.

NEWTONIAN SCIENCE

The outcome of the Enlightenment Period was a vast improvement of living conditions and a vast increase in our knowledge about us and our world. Great advances were made by great scholars in all fields, but especially in the field of physics. The forces of nature were determined and how they worked were framed in mathematical formulas which not only simplified them but made it easy to pass on to other scientists. These forces were worked on by many scientists, but one of the most remarkable was Sir Isaac Newton. He codified some of the forces of nature so everyone could understand them. The first of the forces that we all come in contact with, and thus understand, is electro-magnetism. The second is the weak nuclear force which governs the radioactive decay of elements. The third force is the strong nuclear force which binds the neutrons and protons in the atom's nucleus. The fourth force is gravity, with which we are all familiar because we are all in contact with it all the time. It is this force that Newton worked with and described all its attributes. It is all pervasive and exerting cosmic control on everything found around us in our daily lives, like an apple falling down from a tree, to the way in which our earth circles our sun and satellites circle the earth. With this explosion of knowledge, great progress was made in understanding the workings of our universe. In fact, at one point, around 1900, scientists were claiming that everything in the scientific realm had been discovered and that there was nothing left to be discovered. How wrong they were!

One thing that remained to be done was to combine all the forces into one Unified theory and write it in mathematical terms. Three of the forces had been combined into one comprehensive theory, but the fourth force, gravity, did not lend itself to being added into the unified theory.

While the scientists were working on this problem, a couple of other problems showed up in their research around the turn of the century. One of the problems was the quantum theory. It was a very strange theory with matter doing strange things that do not follow or obey traditional Newtonian physics. It only occurred on very tiny objects. Next there was Einstein's relativity theories that posed more questions than it provided answers. Finally there was the discovery that we had identified less than 10% of the composition of the universe. That meant that we knew nothing about over 90% of the universe's composition. We could not see it, touch it, or anything. All we could do was measure the effect it was having on the small portion of the universe we knew about. The effect was primarily that not only was our universe expanding instead of contracting, as expected, but it was expanding at an increasing rate. The conclusion was that it is caused by this dark matter and energy. This threw scientists into a frenzy, for now all of a sudden, instead of knowing everything about the universe, they knew almost nothing. Today scientists are working feverishly to try to remedy this sudden reversal. They are now questioning their own explanation of dark matter and energy.

Even the age-old knowledge of the atom is now being questioned. Of course, the nucleus of the atom is composed of protons and neutrons, right? Actually no! Besides the protons and neutrons scientists are now finding out that there are also two sub-atomic particles resident in the nucleus of every atom. What is their function? Scientists are again trying to determine the size of the proton; current measurements don't agree with past measurements, and they do not know why or which is correct.

SUMMARY

It seems that we have come full circle, from knowing virtually nothing about our universe, to thinking we know everything about it, and now finding out that we really know virtually nothing about it. This is quite a reversal of thinking. These questions will keep scientists busy for a long time to come.

Some people will think or even assume that this dark material and energy is part the spirit world for which we have been searching. However, I do not believe that this is the case. I think that there is too much interaction between our material world and the dark material. We can even map where the dark material is located and how much is present at each location. That does not sound like separate entities. I think the spirit world is a completely different entity with rules and energy of its own.

So basically, I just wanted to summarize a bit of the present-day world before I started discussing the spirit world.

SECTION III

THE SPIRIT WORLD

INTRODUCTION TO THE SPIRIT WORLD

This is an area about which we know very little, in fact virtually nothing. All we really know comes from various religions and some philosophers who explored this topic. One of the problems associated with these sources is that they vary considerably, thus they are not very reliable. Therefore I will take what seems reasonable from these sources, which will result in a mish-mash of ideas from them plus my own ideas, and hopefully I can combine them into a reasonable presentation.

To my readers, it will appear that I am denigrating the teaching of some religions. Actually if you read carefully, you will note that I am not questioning or denigrating any church, but what I am doing is questioning the various and conflicting interpretations they have about the Bible. Many, if not most, of these interpretations, I believe, were made in the Dark and/or Middle Ages. People were interpreting much older documents and/or stories handed down by word of mouth generation to generation. Some date back to a time even before the Age of Enlightenment or before the time of Jesus, and thus were written or passed down by the people with their particular knowledge and/or understanding of these topics. Perhaps it is time to revisit those interpretations in the light of modern-day knowledge. This is what I have attempted to do in this chapter: i.e. apply today's knowledge and the teachings of Jesus to some of the Old and New Testament teachings.

Many of you are probably wondering why I am questioning the wisdom of the former philosophers and religious experts. Certainly they had the wisdom to explain many of the questions of their time, many of which we still have today. Also in questions about religion, I'm sure they received input from God and/or someone of the spirit world. So why did they end up with such major disagreements in their interpretation of the Bible? I think these misinterpretations are primarily due to their limited understanding of God's creation, namely the universe, and the people He created to inhabit this universe. The Bible was written for all generations of mankind and had to be written to convey His message to all of us. We have made immense progress in the understanding of his creation, so I believe it is necessary for us to reinterpret his Bible to include this new knowledge. I am also sure that, just like in the past, God and the spirit world will guide us in this effort. I have made an effort in this section (Section III) of this book to do just that. Certainly this is not the last word, but I hope it is a beginning.

TABLE OF CONTENTS

CREATING HUMANITY

I brought up two conflicting theories about the origin of the human race. Neither of them proved satisfactory to me since they did not cover the combining of the spirit portions of human beings with the physical portion. I suspect that when God breathed into Adam's nose, it was most likely the spirit entering Adam. Also, it could be interpreted as using Adam as a symbol for all humans, and when he breathed the spirit into Adam, He actually breathed the spirit into all mankind living at that time, and they all became humans with a soul. That item is very important to my way of thinking since I do not consider someone to be a human being until the two are joined. When, how, and if Eve was ever joined with a spirit is still a question. However, I suspect that since she was said to have been created from Adam, who did have a spirit joined with him that was saying that she thus also had the spirit being within her. Also, we could assume that when she was created, at some point she must have taken her first breath, at which time the spirit could have entered her, or she received it when God breathed in to Adam's nostril and all living mankind, including Eve, received the spirit. In any event, we can be sure she was a complete human being (body and soul combined) else why would Adam have chosen her over all the other choices with which he was presented?

The problem with the two theories of creation is the transference of the DNA changes that occurred during the time that Homo sapiens started inhabiting the world to the time the Bible states that Adam appeared on this earth. This would be the inclusion of DNA from the Neanderthals and other human-like species who died out before the appearance of Adam. Thus we are back to our timing problem. My idea that all humans received the spirit at the same time would resolve this problem. Also, I think that the writers of the Old Testament had no concept of time in the billions, millions, or even tens of thousands of years. Also, according to the

Bible, people may have lived a lot longer then, although we do not know why this would be so, but it could introduce another source of error in its account, but not nearly enough to account for the discrepancy. There also seems to be some disagreement in the Bible as to when the animals were created, before or after Adam. So my take on all this is that the Bible account is probably relevant, but with some errors caused by the writers' lack of knowledge of the universe and their use of symbolism, which we really don't understand, to describe events.

FREE WILL AND CHARACTER

Free will! Here we have another item with a lot of references in the Bible and even more in commentaries by religious and philosophical writers. However, most people disagree as to what the Bible really says or means. Is it any wonder that we are all confused by all of this rhetoric? It seems that most of the discussion and confusion comes from whether there really is free will for man or if we really have determinism by God. Then there are the writers who support some kind of hybrid of the two philosophies. If we follow the theory that there really is no free will and meaning that everything is predetermined by God, wouldn't that mean that He is also directly responsible for suffering and evil in this world? Of course, if everything were due to free will, then God would have no control over what happens in this world. So let us look at what that means and what is the most likely and logical answer.

Evidently, when God created man (Adam) the concept of free will was included with this creation. He placed them in the Garden of Eden which included a test for them (the tree of life) where they would have to exercise their free will. This was a gift and a test which He did not grant to any other of His creations. Thus, while He allowed this situation to occur, it was not preordained that Adam and Eve would fail the test. They chose failure of the test using their own free will. My take on the purpose of free will may sound a bit strange, but it sounds more reasonable and logical than many of the other explanations I've read.

When God created man, He created man in His own image, but not as a God. However, He wanted this special creation to be able to become godlike and thus be unable to sin. This must be why He gave man the special gift of free will. It is only by using this free will that man could shed his ability to sin, thus being saved and becoming godlike. Man must use his free will over and over to select the correct way of life until choosing it becomes the normal and only way for him; he will not be able choose the wrong way. The correct way becomes so ingrained in his character that he will be unable to choose the wrong way. Only then can man be saved and join God in heaven. This is why it is such a terrible thing when someone takes away another's free will through physical means, with the use of drugs or whatever means. Their use can have unexpected results. Character is what really distinguishes man from animal. Character is a complex interaction between the physical being and the spirit part of the being. The physical part being supplies some character traits via the genes inherited from his parents and the experiences one has. The spirit part provides the desired long term character attributes and the framework of character's desired result. This would be the end result that the person would be working toward. The physical part has the free will to determine what will actually be done; thus the two may not be in synch, which may be able to cause mental problems, missed opportunities, and questionable behavior. Thus, we sometimes can have an internal battle between the two parts of a human being. Actually this is a very complex area, and I will defer trying to explain it until later, when I publish my follow-up work.

SIN

The first question would be, what is sin?   In the Catholic Church definitions suggest that sin is the breaking of God's or the church's laws, and that there are two levels of sin: mortal, which is a serious sin, and venial, which is a less serious sin. Actually, when going to Confession, it didn't seem to matter what kind of sins one had; they were all forgiven, and the sinner often ended up with the same penance. I never did figure that out. To do it any differently, the seriousness of each sin would have to be judged, and only God can do that, so perhaps there really wasn't any alternative for our form of confession.

Perhaps a better definition of sin would be: anything one does that will separate him further from God. Any of these sins can be classified as being very bad or of a more minor importance depending on the following: How badly did the sin separate the person from God, what was the status of the sinner's mind and heart when he decided to commit the sin, and how intense was the temptation that caused the person to sin? These are things that only God can determine, so he is the only one that can judge. No one else, including man himself, can even judge himself, although he can probably have some idea of the seriousness of the sin he committed. I have read that God can and probably does forgive any sin man commits except for one. That is the sin of rejecting Him as his God, or even of being God. That makes sense in so far as how can He forgive a sin that completely rejects him as a God. So what happens to all sins one commits or as far as that goes, what happens to the good deeds he performs?

THE BOOK OF LIFE

This topic is somewhat confusing and the Bible does not clear it up, at least in my mind. Thus it will take a lot more thought to sort it out. As I see it, when the spirit departs the body and carries with it, the character of that person, as it was developed during his lifetime. This character record is used when the spirit enters the spirit world to determine that spirits future on the spirit world. It seems like the Book of Life is used by God during the final judgment. I don't know if the spirits character record is used in determining the final judgement or just used in the initial judgement'

SUFFERING AND EVIL

Why does God allow suffering and evil for His creation in the world He created? This is a very difficult concept for most of us to accept or even understand. Let us start with God's creation of man. He created man in the image of God, but not as a god. Man still had the ability and opportunity to choose the wrong way, in other words the ability to sin. Of course, a god could not do this. God also told His new creation, "man," that he could actually come to heaven as a reward for overcoming sin. However, to attain this, man must elevate himself to the point where he could not choose the wrong way (sin) as some of His angels had done. To attain that level, He had to provide man with a path or the means to do this. This is how I believe He accomplished it.

God's gift to mankind, and it was not given to any other of His creations, is the gift of "free will." It is this gift that would enable human beings to actually become like God, but not God. The continual use of this gift to choose right over wrong will in time make it impossible for man to choose wrong. This is the path God provided human beings to attain the elevated state to become like God. In order to provide mankind with the opportunities to exercise free will, He had to allow suffering and evil in their lives. This sounds simple enough; however, to be fair about the whole concept, He had to institute protections and limitations for everyone, which were different for each of us. This whole concept is quite complicated and I will defer coverage of it for a future writing.

JUDGEMENT

This is a tough chapter to write, not only because it is a difficult subject about which to write, but also because there are so many entries in the Bible concerning judgement, and many of them seem to disagree with each other. Therefore, I decided to simply write what I believe and sometime when I have the time, I can cross-reference it with the Bible. This will probably get me in trouble with some Bible purists, but I believe as a whole, the Bible is probably misinterpreted in quite a few places.

The Bible states, "Many are called but few are chosen" (Math 22:14). Most likely this refers to the judgement which occurs right after we die; that is the only time it makes sense. God created man and gave him a special gift, free will, which we would have to use to become godlike and to join God in heaven. Since man was His greatest creation, He would hardly allow so few to come to heaven and join Him. Not only does that not make sense, but it is also not logical. He must have provided a path to allow most of His creation to join Him in heaven. Perhaps not all of the following is in the Bible, except for the idea of hell, but this is what many were taught. For example, there was this place called Limbo, which is where all unbaptized persons and the holy ones who lived and died before Christ, went after they died. These Holy Ones were allowed to enter heaven only after Christ opened the gates of heaven. I don't remember if those who died without being baptized ever got the opportunity to leave Limbo. Either way, I do not believe that God would punish these people, such as babies who had no say or chance to be baptized; neither would He punish those who had never even heard of baptism. It just doesn't make sense that He would punish these people; it is not even logical. This would not be the teaching of Jesus Christ. His goal was and is to save most, if not all, of his creation. A second place man could go to for preparing for eternal life with God, according to some religions, is purgatory. This is a place that supposedly uses punishment to purify man so that he may enter heaven. I think it also has fire but not as intense as hell does and it is not everlasting. Once purgatory has purged a being of his sins and adequately punished him, he will be allowed to enter heaven. I doubt that the being can enter heaven immediately, but may have to wait for the final judgement; if so what does he do in the meantime? Again, purgatory is not mentioned directly in the Bible, but has many references that may point to the existence of a purgatory. So how about the argument among Christian churches that man can be saved by faith alone while others say that faith alone will not save one, but that he must also do good deeds to be saved? Is this really an important distinction? We will look at this item again later.

There is one more concept to discuss, namely the question of being "born again." There seems to be a twofold problem here: understanding the various references to it in the Bible and trying to tie them together, and secondly, interpreting them, as to the real meaning of the phrase. It appears that all the churches are correct in their interpretation that it does not mean a physical rebirth of the human body. That would not make sense and is not logical. The combination of genes that created the person, plus the environment that helped develop the personality, only occurred once and could probably not happen again, even by chance, thus ruling out that interpretation. There are a lot of people who profess to have been born again. Looking at the lives some of them lead, it seems hard to see that many of them are really leading Christian lives. Are most of them, or any of them, going to go directly to heaven when they face the first judgment? That is questionable. Being saved requires that man exercise his free will to the point where he cannot choose the wrong way. Perhaps Mother Teresa was one of these people. Perhaps she was born again according to the present definition, I really don't know, but how many can measure up to her?   So we must ask the question, is our interpretation of "born again" correct?   All these differences between churches are actually differences in their Bible interpretations or even merely differences of opinion. Neither is serious enough to cause the separation of the Christians.

EXAMINATION OF CONCEPTS

Let us start out with limbo. First of all, it is not expressly mentioned in the Bible, at least as far as I could determine. There are nevertheless places in the Bible that could be interpreted as references to a place called limbo. They do not clear up the concept of limbo but just seem to muddy the waters even more. In looking at the history of the concept by the various churches, it seems to me that scholars were trying to make sense about something about which they knew nothing and really had no guidance. All they really accomplished was to confuse the issue more for the faithful. So is there something called limbo? Since we really don't know, after thousands of years of discussing it, if there is a limbo, much less what it is, and does it really matter if we believe or not? This continued arguing only perpetuates the division among Christians and doesn't help anyone.

Next, let us look at the concept of there being a place called purgatory. Again, purgatory does not seem to be directly mentioned in the Bible, but there are some references that could be inferring a place called purgatory. Some churches define this as an intermediate place that humans go at their death to be purified so that they can become godlike and enter heaven. This really does not agree with Biblical teaching. According to the Bible, humans are not directly cleansed of their sins by fire or suffering, but gain heaven by exercising their God-given free will.

Even hell, which most or all Christians believe exists and is said to be a pit of everlasting fire, is questionable. I don't think the word for hell is explicitly mentioned in the Bible, but the idea of hell is mentioned using words other than hell. However, none of them seem to translate to what we define hell to be. Our idea of hell as a pit of everlasting fire seems to have come from later Christian writers. There are several problems associated with this concept. First of all, fire was probably the worst punishment that people could imagine and thus became the central theme of hell as a punishment. However, hell is where the spirit of sinners go, not the corporal body. The spirit would not feel fire as we know it; thus, it could not serve as punishment. Some modern theologians consider this fire as a fire in the spirit's feeling/knowledge caused by the realization that they will be separated from God forever. However, that explanation also has some problems. I think hell is probably the complete disappearance of that spirit, and it will not be remembered by anyone for the rest of eternity. I suspect that that would probably be the worst punishment possible. Also, it would fit in with the concept that God is all merciful, whereas an everlasting fire would not fit in with a merciful God

Another major problem is the concept of being "born again." Again, I think the main problem here is the misinterpretation of the Bible. Many people either do not believe in the concept or think it happens while we are living on this earth. I don't think either of these beliefs helps us in any way, so I suspect there must be another explanation of it. I like the saying in the Bible that states we must be born again of the spirit. Now that makes sense to me and solves several problems.

The Bible has quite a few references to "born again," but they don't seem to support each other and just confuse the issue. Historically, the interpretation of these references has changed with time, further confusing the issue. Today the issue is even more confusing since a lot of Christian denominations seem to interpret and practice it differently. So what am I to think of this?

Personally I think that there is something to being "born again," but I do not think it is what we seem to think it is. I think it is a lot more important than we consider it, but we have not yet grasped the true meaning of it. I will defer additional discussion of this concept and cover it in a later publication of mine.

Another point of contention among the various Christian denominations is the different beliefs about saints and the infallibility of the Pope. This has caused some severe splits among Christians. Let us look at the question of saints first. I don't know if the various denominations of Christianity select or venerate saints differently or even have the same saints, but the main source of contention seems to be how they, or if they, venerate the Blessed Virgin Mary, the mother of Jesus.   A greater source of disagreement is the Pope. Many do not believe that he is infallible, which is the teaching of the Catholic Church. This has been a problem and a source of division among Christians for centuries. Should this really be serious enough to cause a major split in the Christion church, or just an agreement to agree to disagree? We should be able to come up with some way that will satisfy everyone. How did the apostles and the early Church Fathers resolve their differences?

PHYSICAL AND SPIRIT WORLD INTERACTION

I don't think there is any interaction between the physical world and the spirit world as far as physical matter is concerned. That, however, is not true for spirits and human beings. It seems to be a one way street, spirit to physical, but not physical to spirit; although human beings may request assistance from the spirit world, they cannot influence the operations of the spirit world. I know of no examples where physical matter entered the spirit world. For those who claim that they saw heaven, or met with God or Jesus or someone in heaven, it seems that it was always their spirit that made the transfer to the spirit world, and as far as I know, no one ever claimed that their physical body traveled with them.

As far as I know, we have had numerous reports of sighting or communication with spirit beings. Some of these, such as ghosts or other apparitions, are most likely some kind of beings from the spirit world or some could be tricks our mind plays on us. However, I do believe there are ghosts and other spirits traveling to the physical world, for whatever reason, and these could be good or evil spirit beings. Some people even believe that there are some spirits living in the physical world if they were not properly released from their physical counterpart.

There are two main ways that the physical world and the spirit world interact.

1. The spirit being provides the physical being with information which requires or requests that the physical being takes some action.

An example of this occurred when I was tricked into attending a party which I had previously decided not to attend. Shortly after arriving at the party I determined that I was there for one reason only, to be used and abused. The first thing the party goers did was to make sure I didn't know what was happening and that I would never remember what happened. I further determined that we were only in phase I of the abuse. Phase II was to occur later, and that would be worse. Shortly before phase II was to start, everyone retreated into a back room to get things organized or something. Somehow they messed up and didn't leave anyone to watch me: thus I was all alone for a short time. For certain reasons I was not planning on leaving the party yet, but as soon as I was all alone, I headed for the door and left the party. Although there were quite a few people attending the party, only four of them planned and directed the flow of the party and knew what happened and why it happened. I have been in contact with those four people and to this day, years later, they have absolutely refused to talk to me. They refuse to talk to me about the party or answer my questions concerning the party. I don't know why I left the party, but I suspect it was due to the intervention of either my Guardian Angel or perhaps some other spirit being interceding for me. I really don't know what spirit being it was.

2.   The spirit being provides the physical being with information which is not known to the physical being.

I also experienced this type of contact with a spirit being two times. The first incident was about two weeks before my mother passed away. Although I was not told explicitly that my mother would pass away shortly, I knew her time had come. The other time occurred on the day before my father passed away. It was on a Sunday thus I was at home rather than at work. I strongly felt that I would never see my father again. The next morning my wife got the call that he had passed away, and she came to my office to notify me.

I don't know why I needed to know the facts I was told, but I'm sure there must have been a reason. There may have been more contacts to me from the spirit world, but none that I can specifically pinpoint.

However, contact by the spirit world with the physical world seems to be quite common. There are mediums and others, including some charlatans I'm sure, who claim they get in contact with spirit beings quite often; however, I suspect that it is normally the spirit beings that actually make the initial contact, after the physical being requests the contact. I suspect that some maintain that they make the initial contact, and perhaps they do.

God does not interfere with man's free will very often and then only for a good reason. One reason may be that both sides are not capable of handling the incident, so for the good of both sides He may interfere with the planned incident. Another reason may be that he has future plans for one or the other or both the participants, and therefore He spares one or both participants; thus, He may not allow the planned incident to occur.

LIFE IN THE SPIRIT WORLD

So what happens to us when we die? Actually death can be defined as happening when the spirit part of us departs from our physical being. Scientists, doctors, and theologians have been trying to define when death occurs for a long time without too much success. Some define it as happening when the heart stops beating, others define it as when brain waves cease, but neither explanation seems to hold true all the time. The only consistent explanation seems to be when the spirit departs from the physical being. However, we have no way of determining as to when that happens, so we are left with uncertainty as to when death actually occurs.

In any case, when death does occur, the spirit departs from the physical body. The spirit then departs the physical world and enters the spirit world. There are some who believe the spirit does not always depart the physical world, but remains for some reason or other, but it does depart from the physical being. I currently have no explanation for this phenomenon or what it does if it remains in the physical world.

However, when the spirit departs the physical world and enters the spirit world, what happens to it, and what does the spirit do? I suppose that this is when the initial judgement occurs. To a large extent the result of this initial judgment determines what happens to them. Some would say that they normally go to a place of punishment, such as purgatory, to atone for their sins. However, I do not believe that a merciful God would choose punishment as a way of atoning for sins and especially not for teaching mankind right from wrong. Since God created man in His likeness and gave man the special gift of "free will" as the path to salvation, why would He not use this as a way to teach man right from wrong? I'm sure He would have man use free will to learn right from wrong rather than punishment. So how does He do this, since free will seems to be a gift to physical mankind, not spirits? This is another large topic which I will not attempt to resolve in this book but will have to do in a later writing.

I will not try to define the functions, etc. in which the spirits of human beings are involved in the spirit world. However, I will say that an important function will be to reconcile the differences between human beings which developed while they were resident in the physical world. These differences must be reconciled before they can enter heaven and be with God. While these differences probably can be reconciled in the spirit world, it would be much easier and better to reconcile them before we leave the physical world since they are a product of the physical world. I will have more on this subject in a later writing.

CONCLUSIONS AND RECOMMENDATIONS

So, what have we done to Christianity? Over two thousand years ago, Christ started the Christian church; he started one Christian church, not hundreds of them. He created a single church to assist his flock in saving themselves, to assist them in doing this most important task. He must now be "turning over in his grave," as one of our sayings goes. How sad Christ must be when He looks down on actions of His flock! How could they have strayed so far from the path He provided before he departed this earth? I think it is time we determine how we strayed so far and what we can do to remedy it. First, we will look at the problems between the church denominations and determine how we can remedy them. I'm certain that I won't get close to listing all of them, but these can be a good start and perhaps point the way to remedy all of them. It would certainly be worth a try and is something we must do now, rather than later. First of all, we need to stop emphasizing the differences between the churches and start emphasizing the common elements of the churches. It is the common elements that make us Christians, not our differences. We have made it too easy for anyone to create a new Christian church for their own purposes, including making money and tax evasion. Also, regular Christian churches are entering the business area to evade taxes and make money. It is giving Christianity a bad name and this is not Christian living.

There are certain differences that are rather superfluous, like the belief in limbo and purgatory. These items, and I'm sure many others, are not even directly mentioned in the Bible and separate the various factions in the way the factions have interpreted passages which do or sound like they refer to some of our practices. Does it really matter how we interpret these passages we really don't know anyway? Basically, most of us really don't know, much less understand, the Bible, so does it really matter if we don't agree on something we don't understand, and thus does not affect how we worship or live our lives? Let's save the discussions for the important concepts, not the trivial. I know some people will say that we must follow the Bible to the letter even if we don't understand it; however, that usually means we follow their interpretation of the Bible. We could even add hell to the list since it has some of the same problems as limbo and purgatory has.

The argument of faith vs. deeds is also a questionable argument. We are really saved by using our free will to choose the correct way, and that will mean using our free will to have faith in God and using our free will to do good deeds. Thus, the two items are really the end result of exercising our free will correctly.

Sainthood is also a non-argument. Now various denominations have established procedures, although they vary between the various denominations, to determine who is a saint. However, I don't think that the early church had any set procedure for selecting who would be a saint. Do we really know what a saint is?

The power of the Pope is even more controversial and has caused and is maintaining splits between Christians. The main problem seems to be the infallibility of the Pope when he speaks on articles of faith. Again, it involves an interpretation of the Bible. Some, like the Catholics, say it is definitely in the Bible; others say it is only a misinterpretation of a Biblical statement. So who is correct? I don't know if these all are in matters of faith or what, but the bottom line is, that if the Pope issues a statement, Catholics think it must be the truth, whether it is a matter of faith or not. There is also a question as to what happened during the time period when we had two popes? These are valid questions for those who question the Pope's authority.

How about the matter of being born again? This is a strange concept since some Christian denominations don't even talk about it; they just ignore the concept. A lot of denominations not only believe in it, but say we must be born again to be saved. However, I don't know if there is much of any difference between those who say they were born again and those who were not born again. Perhaps it is more of a talking point or a badge of honor than a tenet of faith. I think this is just another one of those points where it doesn't matter what you believe, so why are we letting it divide us?

Looking at all those concepts that are dividing us, most or perhaps all could be resolved by applying a few simple rules. First, decide which ones are trivial differences that really do not affect our faith in Christianity; let us discard them for they are of no consequence. Second, decide which ones are merely differences in how we interpret the Bible. Set them aside since we probably cannot determine who is correct anyway, so why waste time arguing about them and let them continue to separate us? And finally, "agree to disagree." Isn't that what we essentially have done anyway, except we also allowed it to separate us, making it almost impossible to reconcile?

I know these recommendations will have everyone up in arms, denouncing me for asking them to give up their most cherished Bible beliefs. Actually, nobody is being asked to relinquish any of their beliefs unless they want to do that of their own volition. The only ones they may agree to give up are those they have determined are not important enough to argue over or separate us. Items of Biblical interpretation are either resolved or become items about which we "agree to disagree."I truly believe that in time we will come together on more and more of these items and eventually

become a true Christian Church. Christians can maintain their belief in any church they wish and fulfill their obligations. They will gather together and be able to discuss their religion without concern that they are doing wrong. We will be enjoying true Christianity.

Perhaps my biggest concern in living our everyday lives as Christians is the fact that we are not living Christian lives; in fact, some of us are living heathen lives; we could care less about our fellow humans. Just take a look at Facebook and our other social media outlets. There we throw together Christian value postings with postings asking for the death or imprisonment of our political enemies or demeaning them. We undermine another person's character with little or no regard for truth. We believe we can print anything we wish and believe it is the person's responsibility to prove that they are innocent. The posting party truly believes they have no responsibility to just print the facts, Does this sound like Christianity? It is actually sickening to read some of the social media postings.

As far as my recommendation go, I would recommend that we must do our best to unify Christianity into one church as it was meant to be. Only if we are unified will the rest of the world look up to Christianity as a way of life they will follow. As a religion broken into many pieces and often at odds with each other, people tend to shy away from Christianity and to look elsewhere for direction or just plain ignore it. In fact, I think Christianity is losing ground.

If I were the one to unify Christianity, I would start with two major factions of Christianity: the Roman Catholic Church and the Orthodox Church. I think that this was probably the first major split of the Christian Church, so the leaders of these two factions should get together to resolve their differences in accordance with the guidelines mentioned earlier. Once these two have united, the rest of the sects would see the good that has come from unification and would follow suit. In the meantime, the various factions of the Lutheran Church, for example, and also various factions of the Baptist Church could each get together and resolve their differences, and each could present a united front when talking to a unified Christian church to combine with it.

First let me assure you, I am not an expert on religion or Christianity; in fact, I can barely say that I am a novice. I have never spent much time studying either area. Everything I know is from living in a country we say is Christian, but we don't seem to live like Christians, and doing a lot of thinking about what Christianity really is.. We pay little attention to God, and we don't act like Christians to our neighbors; in fact, we usually don't know who our neighbors are but we do hope and just hope they are the same color and believe the same things we do. We judge them, try to punish them our way, and if all else fails, we slander them.

All of my ideas are based on two characteristics of God and considering these two characteristics, how would He have interpreted the Bible? These two characteristics are first, as we saw in section 2 of this book, God is extremely logical. Why would He deviate from His logic when designing the book that is our blueprint for living? Second, He is all merciful as was extremely evident when He sent His Son to live among us. Why would He deviate from His merciful personality when designing the book that is to be our blueprint for living? I do not believe people used these guidelines when reading and interpreting the Bible. I tried to make these two characteristics the center point of my interpretation of the Bible. The Unified Christian Church would have to be in sync with the two most important commandments which Christ gave us, namely "to love God above all" and "love our neighbor as ourselves." Also, in defining what true Christianity is, its definition must follow Christ's important two commandments "Thou shalt love

the Lord thy God with all thy heart, and with all thy
soul, and with all thy mind. This is the first and great
commandment. And the second is like unto it, "Thou
shalt love thy neighbor as thyself." Without adhering
to these two commandments, we do not have
Christianity.

How about the non-Christian people of this world? Why
would they ever want to become Christians? They look at
the Christian people and all they see is our corrupt way of
living non-Christian lives. They think money and power
have become our God. We drink, gamble, often don't keep
the Sabbath holy, squander our resources and money on
meaningless and sinful purposes, let crime and even murder
run rampart, and demean our friends and neighbors. So, why
should they seek to become Christians? If we began to live
Christian lives, I think that they would seek to join us.

Perhaps this is what bothers me: trying to become a kinder
and gentler people while being such poor Christians. We
must make progress mainly because the alternative is
unthinkable. If we don't change our ways, world conditions
will continue to deteriorate, perhaps forcing us to rethink the
way we live.

FINAL SUMMATION

We have come to the end of the book; thus the time has come for the final summation/recommendation. We can implement all of the recommendations I have made, but will that solve all of our problems? Not immediately, but if enough of us desire this change, we can make it happen. We are so engrained with our current lifestyle, we really seem to have no desire to change it, unless things get so bad that we have no other choice but to change our lifestyle. Of course, we do have a choice; we can decide to change and become a kinder and gentler people at any time and perhaps save us a lot of heartache and pain. But will a significant majority if us decide to change and thus change the world? Only time will tell.

CONTACT INFORMATION

Additional copies of this book can be obtained on-line from Amazon.com. Another one of my publication *The Depression Kid Grows Up* is also available from Amazon.

I have established a special e-mail address which you can use to contact me regarding comments or questions pertaining to this book. I will attempt to answer as many of your e-mails as possible:

douglasschroeder100@gmail.com